THE PHILOSOPHY OF RIGHT

*****

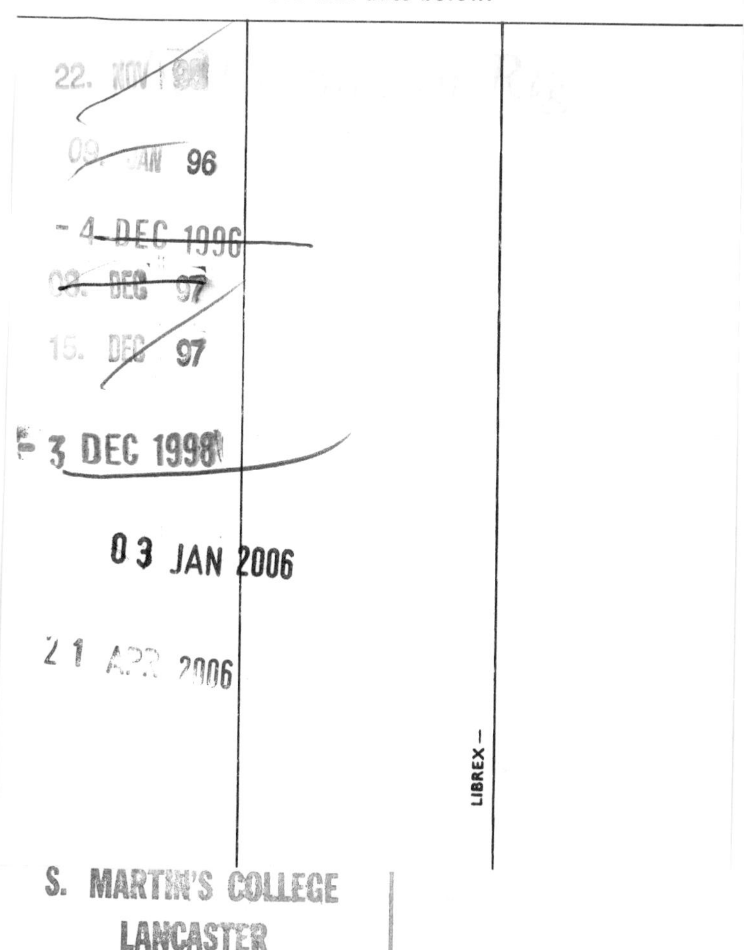

ANTONIO ROSMINI

THE PHILOSOPHY OF RIGHT

Volume 1

Introduction - Moral System

The Essence of Right

Translated by

DENIS CLEARY

and

TERENCE WATSON

ROSMINI HOUSE
DURHAM

Rosmini House, Woodbine Road
Durham DH1 5DR, U.K.

Translated from
Filosofia del Diritto
Vol. I, Intra, 1865

Typeset by Rosmini House, Durham
Printed by Bell & Bain Limited, Glasgow

ISBN 0 9513211 7 X

Note

Square brackets [ ] indicate notes or additions by the translators.

[. . .] indicates an omission from the text.

References to this and other works of Rosmini are given by paragraph number unless otherwise stated.

Paragraph numbers in this volume are the work of the translators.

Abbreviations used for Rosmini's quoted works are:

AMS: *Anthropology as an Aid to Moral Science*
CE: *Certainty*
CS: *Conscience*
PE: *Principles of Ethics*
SP: *Society and its Purpose*
SC: *The Summary Cause for the Stability or Downfall of Human Societies*

Foreword

In this foreword we want to indicate the point already reached in our series of English translations of Rosmini's philosophical works, justify the next immediate step forward, and illustrate the principles underlying Rosmini's philosophy of right.

The works already available in English[1] offer a general view of Rosmini's treatment of the principles of knowledge (*The Origin of Thought*, *Certainty*), of the principles of morality and their final application (*Principles of Ethics* and *Conscience*), and of the basic realities comprising the human being, that is, the feeling, intellective and moral subject (*Anthropology as an Aid to Moral Science*). Together, these volumes provide a fairly complete conspectus of the fundamental elements of human nature and its moral action. Without these works, it would be impossible to refer in English to explanations of tenets which Rosmini uses consistently throughout the whole of his philosophical production.

This does not mean that the books presented so far are the only works available in the Rosminian corpus on epistemology, anthropology and morality. In particular, Rosmini's historical analysis of the development of ideas in these subjects still awaits translation,[2] together with his fully developed notions on the human subject.[3] For the moment, however, we have turned our attention to another field of philosophy in order to make best use of what is already available and apply it to a matter of intense interest and importance in our own day.

It is not perhaps exaggerated to state that human rights — their nature, existence, development, exercise and protection — have been

(1) *The Origin of Thought*, 2nd edition, Durham, 1989.
Principles of Ethics, 2nd edition, Durham, 1989.
Conscience, Durham, 1989.
Certainty, Durham, 1992.
Anthropology as an Aid to Moral Science, Durham, 1992.

(2) Cf. especially, the first volume of *Nuovo Saggio sull'origine delle idee*, Intra, 1875, and *Storia comparativa e critica de' sistemi intorno al principio della morale*, Intra, 1867.

(3) Cf. *Psicologia*, vols 1-4, critical edition, Stresa 1988-89.

the most debated subject of the past decade. This affirmation would certainly be true if we could judge the quantity and quality of debate by the conviction with which human rights are either asserted and valued or gratuitously invented in our daily existence and in the corridors of power. Let us say, therefore, that problems regarding the exercise of human rights are at least at the forefront of popular and philosophic discussion.

Listening to the discussion, as everyone must who pays the slightest attention to the world at large, we find ourselves embroiled (it is not too strong a word) in a confusion of ideas and thoughts that offers no possibility of cohesion and development on a theoretical plane, and total absurdity in practice. The spectrum of action runs from the defence of animal rights to 'ethical cleansing', whose sole justification is a high-sounding phrase concealing a great evil; the spectrum of theory embraces systems making positive law the source of rights, and systems that deny the existence of rights which cannot be sanctioned by might.

The interest in human rights has not been repaid, it would seem, by any coherent, global thought. Everyone is convinced of the existence, necessity and importance of human rights, but there is no underlying foundation of principle enabling us, practitioners of these rights, to understand and evaluate them. We continue to insist upon the gravity of the problem, at least when there is question of our own rights, but we do not understand scientifically where the essence of rights lies, nor how rights are activated, exercised and supported in our daily lives. This lack of a sound, philosophical basis on which to build the edifice of rights leads inevitably to yet another fulfilment of words spoken long ago: the house is built 'upon the sand; and the rain fell, and the floods came, and the winds blew and beat against that house and it fell; and great was the fall of it.' As we look around the world, near and far, we can only marvel at the contradiction between our interest in human rights and the appalling treatment meted out in practice to possessors of rights.

Nevertheless, unfailing human instinct for the preservation of rights will not allow them to fall into oblivion. Despite neglect and abuse of rights, people know in practice and will insist that they are of supreme importance. The almost totally non-violent overthrow of communism in Eastern Europe, the suspicions felt about signs of totalitarianism wherever it manifests itself, the growing feeling for the unshakeable personal value of the handicapped and ailing, and even the preservation of the jury system and its commonsense approach to things, are all signs that human rights are not forgotten amongst ordinary people. In great things and small, we all understand what is meant when we utter or hear the cry: 'It's not fair.' Whether we are able to express our understanding is another matter.

What then do we mean by human rights? This is the problem addressed by Rosmini in his *Philosophy of Right*, the sheer size of which[1] is indicative of the nature of the difficulties found in the question. Rosmini's answer takes us through a study of the essence of right, the derivation of rights, rights of the individual, social right and, within social right, the rights of the family, the Church and the State. The aim is always to point the way to the foundation of laws on the single principle of justice. In this first English volume, we find Rosmini dealing with the essence of right and the derivation of rights, both of which will be explained briefly in this foreword.

But is an explanation needed? Can we not leave Rosmini to provide his own explanation? We could, but Rosmini's wordiness, his engagement with the philosophical problems debated in his own time, and his erudition combine to place obstacles to modern understanding.

Rosmini's diffuseness, immediately obvious in practically all of his works, is not empty verbosity, but the expression of a desire to offer an adequate explanation for everything he says. Unfortunately, this encompasses difficulties which are real enough, but which would not perhaps have occurred to the average reader. Once pointed out, however, they can be seen for what they are. At this stage, the hare is scented, the chase begins and some time elapses before a return can be made to the point under discussion.

This particular difficulty is aggravated when the problem encountered has its roots in the history of the philosophy of right, or is more relevant to Rosmini's time than to our own. History is especially important for Rosmini in this study because it is the source on which he draws for the non-philosophical notion of right which, he maintains, is never lost sight of by human instinct.

[1] *Filosofia del diritto*, vols 1-2 (in all pp. 1777), Intra, 1865. The work, written between 1840 and 1842, was first published in its entirety at Milan in 1845. Other editions followed at Naples in 1847 and 1856. The Intra edition contains the corrections made by Rosmini to the first edition. The author's philosophical acumen is matched in this work, as in others, by his vast erudition and historical insight. About 440 authors are quoted in all, and almost as many laws, most of which are placed firmly and clearly in their historical context.

His knowledge of the history of law, for instance, enables him to show on various occasions that what he upholds philosophically and methodologically is already present in the practice of justice and in legal enactments. His appeals to history are consistently enlightening, but can often serve as a distraction from the main thrust of his argument.

As we said, this difficulty is also relevant to problems which were actual enough for Rosmini but have no implications for ourselves — at least we think they have no importance for us, although in practice every code of law and every civil constitution will depend in some way on what has been enacted and decided in times past. Rosmini deals with such matters at length and in doing so tends once more to distract his readers' thought from the main argument.

Something similar occurs as the reader tries to keep pace with Rosmini's erudition which is always displayed helpfully, but at times superabundantly. At points like this, it too may become a distraction from the basic topic.

Considerations of this kind make it imperative to offer a brief synopsis of the basic principles of each volume of this translation. Here, we deal with justice as the foundation of all law, the philosophy of right as the science of justice, the relationship between right and morality, the definition and the derivation of rights.

Finally, something will have to be said about the choice of certain English words used in expressing Rosmini's thought.

Fiat justitia, ruat coelum (Let justice prevail, whatever the consequences). This must be the first principle underlying all positive law. Justice, says Rosmini, is the first principle of law in the human heart; people never forget that the most simple, basic foundation-notion of all law is justice. Thinkers who abandon human instinct for the sake of their limited reflection may lose sight of justice, but common sense never does. From this premise, substantiated by an accurate analysis of the notion of justice, Rosmini is able to declare that our business, absolutely speaking, is not to make laws, but to interpret the supreme law of justice. Positive laws, he maintains, are to be judged by justice.[1] The implications of this affirmation for natural law concepts, and for the application of natural law to jurisprudence, are profound and lasting. The supreme natural, moral

[1] For the relationship between morality and justice, cf. *Principles of Ethics* and, in the present work, the section entitled *Moral System*, 93-222.

law, expressed in the self-evident precept, 'Love being for what you know it to be', or 'Love being in its order', contains the notion of justice, that is, the requirement that we respect all beings for what they are, and recognise in practice the rights which are theirs. In the end, the philosophy of right will be nothing other than 'the science of justice'. In other words, the philosophy of right will show us in an orderly fashion how justice is the principle of right and the source of all its derivations in various kinds of rights. In this sense, the philosophy of right, considered as the science of justice, stands as the unshaken foundation of every human authority as well as that of every legislation springing from that authority. There is nothing more 'radical' than justice, nothing more subversive of 'unlawful legality' than the philosophy of right. *Fiat justitia, ruat coelum.*

What constitutes the right(s) that justice obliges us to respect? Various definitions of right are offered throughout this first volume of the *The Philosophy of Right*; all of them can be reduced to the following elements:

— useful, personal activity, at least potential activity, on the part of some intelligent being

— moral freedom on the part of the person who exercises his/her activity (in other words, the person must be free, morally speaking, to act as he/she wishes — there is no right to immoral activity)

— moral exigency in others which requires them, on pain of harming another, not to interfere with the exercise of this faculty by the subject possessing moral freedom of action.

It is clear from this briefest of outlines that a right is always a relationship between two intelligent, volitive beings, one of whom is free to act, morally speaking, while the other is obliged to respect, morally speaking, that freedom of action. Examination of the nature of this action and of the respect due to it from others is at the heart of Rosmini's treatise on the essence of right but it is evident from what has been said that right stands half-way between morality and utility. Through his activity, the subject of right must be carrying out something morally upright and good for self; others must respect this activity, which cannot be violated without harm to the subject and consequently without immorality on the part of those offending the subject.

Rosmini goes on to use the five elements forming the supreme principle of right (activity, personal activity, useful activity, upright activity on the part of the subject of right; moral exigency in others not to interfere with the exercise of this faculty of activity) in order to show how rights are derived from the supreme principle. In effect, a right is truly present in an individual or a society when it can be shown that all five elements have their place in some relationship between persons. These elements may be constituted by the very nature of relationships between human beings or be acquired as life goes on. We thus have the two great divisions of right: connatural and acquired rights, which in turn are divided into rights of the individual and rights of society.

The activity to which Rosmini refers as a constituent of right has a general characteristic marking it out as a necessary element of right. This characteristic is ownership, that is, the dominion a person has over something: ownership is 'the strict union of a thing with a person by means of which that thing is reserved totally and exclusively to the person as if it were part of him/her'. How ownership, in the broadest sense of the word, is itself constituted is explained at length by Rosmini. Here, we need simply underline the truth that the violation of rights involves at least an attempt to harm the relationship between a person and what he owns (what is proper to him). In effect, the assailant strikes at the person himself when he attempts to undermine the person's ownership; it is the violation of personship which constitutes the immorality brought about by the violation of rights. From a positive point of view, we may affirm that the living person exists as the source of right and of rights through his activity as a being who is someone and who does something.

Rosmini's philosophy of right is dependent, therefore, on his doctrine of person.[1] This teaching can now be seen as the vital heart of his philosophy of right, providing, as it does, a vision of the human person rooted in subjective feeling and — far more sublimely — determined by the sight of the idea of being, which is the immortal, infinite, necessary light of reason linking us once and for all with our Creator, but without disclosing him as he is in himself. In the last analysis, it is this inviolable light of being that is offended, but not diminished, when the subject of rights is harmed; the same light is denied in and by the assailant when he blinds himself to others' rights and tries to make his own what is already theirs.

So much for the core of this first English volume of *The Philosophy*

[1] Cf. AMS, 832 ss.

of Right. Some remarks about the translation itself must be now added to this introduction.

First, we accept that the use of 'Right' (where right is printed with upper case 'R') is an irritant. Rosmini himself, however, states that his own use of it in Italian is consistent with his desire to refer in such instances to the 'science of Right' rather than to actual rights themselves. We have, therefore, endeavoured to reproduce his usage, although we are not convinced that it is entirely consistent with his stated aim. This may be due either to lapses on Rosmini's part, or to inadequate correction of the complicated galley proofs of the original editions of the work. In passing, we may also mention that Rosmini's use of footnotes has been respected as far as possible. But, as usual in these translations, we have inserted in the Appendix footnotes which would have run over to a second or even third page. Reference to their place in Rosmini's text is clearly indicated.

Second, the unusual word 'jural' has been used for the Italian *giuridico* which, translated as 'juridical', would have given a very restricted and often false idea in English of what was intended. We understand 'jural' in the sense defined by the *Oxford English Dictionary*, that is, 'of or pertaining to rights and obligations'.

Third, the word 'personship' has been used consistently to translate Rosmini's *personalità*. Employing 'personality', now degraded in English to a description of phenomenological characteristics, would inevitably have distracted readers from the metaphysical connotations of Rosmini's use of the word.

DENIS CLEARY
TERENCE WATSON

Durham,
February, 1993.

Contents

INTRODUCTION

MORAL SYSTEM

THE ESSENCE OF RIGHT

It is childish to search for brevity or length when writing laws. My own opinion is that we have to choose neither the shortest nor the longest, but the BEST

Plato, *Laws*, 1: 4.

INTRODUCTION

I.

The importance of the philosophy of right

1. Modern governments, which are under constant pressure to provide definitive, certain and universally applicable legislation, find favour if they succeed in providing codes of law with these qualities. Certainly it would be ungrateful not to acknowledge what has been achieved by governments for the improvement of laws during the last century and up to the present. In my own opinion, I would add to my gratitude a sincere desire that all nations and indeed the whole world achieve the perfect legislation — definitive, certain and universally applicable — for which they long.

Nevertheless, I have to ask why those who desire this admirable kind of legislation never take into account the need to choose between just and unjust legislation. I admit that this kind of problem seems simplistic, and could provoke an angry or mocking reply. It is, of course, obvious that laws should be just; there is nothing new or strange in requiring laws characterised by justice. Nor do I doubt that people realise the need for justice as the primary factor in legislation: I know that when they have just laws they are content. I am puzzled, however, when I see, amidst the clamour for definitive, certain and universally applicable law, that so few people remember to speak about legislation as 'just', or to call it 'just' from the start.

2. Is this too obvious? Is drawing attention to justice too simple and outmoded? People whose sole desire is to say something new and recondite may perhaps be ashamed to repeat what has been maintained throughout the ages as a part of ordinary common sense, but this surely is an unsatisfactory attitude. In any case, I am prepared, even at the risk of appearing simple and out of date, to persist with my enquiries about justice and legislation.

My question is this: is it more important for the laws imposed upon nations, or chosen by them, to be just, or to be certain, definitive and universal? There is no doubt that justice is required above all else, but it is equally true that if laws are just, no other quality is required. Certainty, definitiveness and universality is desirable in laws only because these are conditions of justice; justice requires that laws possess these noble prerogatives. In other words, all the qualities desired for good laws, whatever these qualities may be, are already contained in the basic quality of justice; on the other hand, such qualities do not, of themselves, contain justice.

Dealing with law without expressly discussing justice means rejecting the genuine substance and vital principle of laws and forcing people to look for it elsewhere — perhaps in daily life, or in common sense, or best of all, in human consciousness itself (from which certain kinds of writers wish to dissociate themselves). And we must indeed conclude that the first, most simple and important element in moral and jural disciplines is inserted in all human souls by divine Providence because everyone stands in need of it. It remains in the depth of the spirit, common to all, yet neglected — because too familiar.

3. There are indeed times when writers may legitimately insist less on the most important, radical element of things, and focus more insistently upon the partial derivations and consequences of this element. This can easily be explained by the law of progress to which the human spirit is subject. When attention flags, it is entirely natural for the spirit to pass to other matters connected with the object of its meditation. A thousand stimuli draw the spirit to abandon the object upon which its attention is fixed: the spirit may, for instance, be satisfied with what it knows, or tired of it. Almost all human faculties operate by moving from one act to another, from one object to another, and necessarily draw with them the attention which is their common force. Attention is no longer applied to principles, the original object of reflection, but to consequences. Curiosity and reasoning play their part in this, together with the multiplicity, ingenuity, remoteness and attraction of consequences. The elementary principles from which the spirit has set out are forgotten or neglected. Henceforward the spirit gropes along, deprived of its guiding principles and directed solely by its opinions. These in turn are at the mercy of its passions, which in the end disguise themselves in rational garb by simulating the true principles whose dominion they have usurped.

When the spirit has existed for a long time without genuine principles, however, it comes to realise that it has completely lost its way in an arid, trackless land. Terrified by its state and distrustful of self, it feels deeply its extreme need of the sadly forgotten principles, and longs for them as the deer longs for running water.

The minds of individuals function in this way, and the same path of thought is taken by the collective mind of societies.

4. Some centuries are noted for their principles; in these periods, thought is healthy and strong, but poorly developed. Some centuries combine principles and consequences; thought is still healthy and strong — because principles have not been forgotten — and makes progress. In these periods nations flourish.

Other centuries follow, noted only for consequences. Principles are out of date, cold, boring. They still exist in proverbial form, but no one reflects on them. In these periods, thought, weak as it is, submerges itself in sophistry and frivolity, and connives with the senses. These centuries are lax, superficial, effeminate, corrupt — moments in which nations perish, and humanity offers a poor image of itself. Prouder than ever, humanity despises the stupidity of previous ages and cuts itself off from its fathers. It passes from vanity to vanity, from one abyss to another, and finally finds itself intolerable in its own eyes. But humanity wakens to its own misery and if helped by heaven — to which the broken spirit may have appealed — will perhaps turn back hesitatingly to search for the lost elements of knowledge; it concentrates once more on the first principles, whose immense importance and absolute necessity it begins to appreciate better. The principles become more beautiful, newer, fresher; they reveal themselves more clearly than when first contemplated. The spirit now possesses that reflective attention which returns to concentrate upon principles with a mind strengthened by exercise, with an adult understanding, with a more open, empty and hungry heart.[1] A second unfolding of ages, like the first but broader in its scope, begins for humanity.

[1] These periods, which manifest a law that presides inexorably over the course of nations, are revealed first in different ways of *thinking* amongst peoples in various ages, then in their *affections*, and finally in their external *actions*, all of which go to make up their final expression, the *political state* of society. I have shown elsewhere that the way people think necessarily influences the way they act. The ages which I distinguish here in the speculative

5. Moral and logical principles had already been degraded and rendered obsolete in the eyes of the 17th century, a period when human attention was concentrated on accessories, ceremony, verbal altercations and capricious, extraordinary novelties. Mankind, betrayed by debility of mind, sank into dissoluteness and impiety which in turn brought forth anarchy, and destroyed public order of every kind. Towards the end of the 18th century, people could be seen reaching out for the forgotten principles, but only like drowning sailors grasping at straws in the hope of salvation. The 19th century is destined by Providence to re-establish the importance of true principles, and to make known to future generations the simplicity, supreme importance and incomparable beauty of these principles. If I have understood what is taking place in this present century, and have correctly interpreted its need and desires, people everywhere are secretly intent upon a work which some have already undertaken openly. They seek to return to the simplest principles and use them as the cornerstone of the edifice of human knowledge, virtue, happiness and society.

6. The principles of thought shine in the mind prior to all other cognitions because they are attuned to human nature itself. The great mass of humanity adheres to these principles as it adheres to the most elementary ideas, and continues to give them its adherence while individuals, whose powerful minds make them the avant-garde of mankind, seem to have rejected them. We should not be surprised, therefore, at recent appeals to common sense against the wayward speculation of the learned. Common sense has become a lighthouse erected by Providence on the immovable rock of humankind. Its light shines to guide home those individuals who have ventured too far for safety.

7. This kind of reflection has always directed my thought almost involuntarily in the research to which I have been drawn by the immense consolation found in love of what is true and good. I have felt the need to refer far more to humankind — to

order correspond, therefore, to those which I distinguished elsewhere in the political order. States originate, develop, grow old and perish in so far as they pay attention to principle or lose themselves in accidental and isolated consequences. Cf. *The Summary Cause for the Stability or Dowfall of Human Societies*, cc. 3-7.

the human nature in which we all share (which is God's own work) — than to the sayings of philosophers. There is immense satisfaction, as well as the fulfilment of an obligation, in being a lowly companion and disciple of the great majority of my neighbours; with them I can appreciate more deeply, search more diligently and meditate more lovingly the most common truths, authenticated as it were by a greater number of witnesses.

Hence the principal rule of method that I have employed in the books I have published, and which I intend to use in the present work, is to begin philosophising from what is most simple, obvious and well-known. If I begin with a genuine, indubitable truism, I am sure that I have a firm foundation for my work. I have never regretted following this rule, nor do I regret it now. I have learned that 'the best or highest wisdom is not found in particulars, nor in generalities; it is that which allows the mind to see particulars in what is general.' But the most general of all truths are those which enlighten the minds of the people. Thus the task of knowledge, the height of human wisdom, is to contemplate true particulars in such resplendent truths, where they properly belong.

8. In applying these considerations to positive laws, I became convinced that the most simple, basic, and therefore most noble idea is that of *justice*. All solid attempts at reasoning about positive laws had to begin here. Every other value possessed by positive law appeared accidental, accessory and derivative; the essence of the perfection of laws consisted in justice alone. And it is certain that the mind has to concentrate totally on the essence of what it is thinking about. Arriving at the naked *essence* of anything, it must throw itself upon it and devour it. The essence of anything is like an inexhaustible mine in which the mind can dig endlessly and find only pure gold.

In fact, the simple and altogether general ideas which we indicated as lights enkindled in human nature by the Creator are precisely the essences of those superior realities required by human nature. And one of these essences is justice.

The profoundly mistaken thought that abandons these essences, and the ambitious discourse that excludes them, drifts around in search of what is already possessed. The forms taken by such thought and discourse may sound eminently scientific and highly persuasive, but they are substantially useless. The core of truth is lacking, and humankind, expecting great things, harvests wind alone.

9. But I began with a question about the certainty, definitiveness and universality of the laws governing civilised nations. The philosophers and publicists to whom I directed it are sound, of course, when they correctly require these qualities in laws. However, they take for granted the question of justice; justice is present as it were of its own accord. If I were to press my question, and ask them about the nature of this justice, which all agree is so necessary that there is no need to speak about it, they would probably come to blows over the answer — although not before turning on me to mock my plebeian question. Some of them would certainly want to tell me that justice is simply what is *useful*, and is nothing more than self-interest properly understood. This would be denied by others who find themselves without any idea of justice at all.

At this point it should be clear why utilitarians spend so much effort and care speaking about the beautiful qualities that laws should have, but take very little notice of justice. For them, the word has no content; 'justice' can be taken for granted because it has become a mere synonym for utility.

10. A little thought will show the real reason why modern writers spend so little time discussing justice, and expand so much effort considering the exterior and logical form of laws, their outward expression, their suitability and the political reasons motivating them. For such utilitarians, or those who care only for what is useful, justice is a kind of wound that should barely be touched; higher matters can be scrutinised as though they were completely cut off from justice.

At the height of its powers, the previous century lost sight of justice, the essence of the perfection of laws. Attention was confined to utility; principles were replaced by consequences. Justice is a *principle*; utility is a *consequence*. While utility as a consequence is considered in its connection with the principle of justice, thought remains sound; when utility alone attracts the spirit's attention, sophistry reigns in minds and anarchy in society. Laws are looked at from an exterior point of view, wholly extraneous to their true, intimate essence.

11. This movement of the spirit's attention towards utility and

away from the justice proper to laws is not an isolated fact. The human spirit took the same step at every level of thought in the last two centuries.

The following general formula expresses the condition of the mind when it has abandoned the contemplation of what is essential in order to devote itself exclusively to what is accessory: 'People reject ideas, and devote their attention to sensations alone.' Sensism: this is the single word explaining everything that has happened in theory and in practice. Sensism is a synonym of *crass stupidity*, a common phenomenon of presumptuous, verbose humanity. Only ideas indicate essences; sensations, which are nothing at all without ideas, are simply accessories for the intelligent subject. Utility is a fact, as sensation is a fact; justice is an idea. Beholding the facts in this idea of justice is to behold 'particulars in what is general'. This is the human wisdom of which we were speaking; and this is the aim of the *philosophy of Right*.

12. In my ideological works, I undertook a general examination of modern *sensism* and its consequence, *subjectivism*. My starting point was the ordinary phrase, 'the light of reason',[2] which I tried to clarify. In the same way, I want to start from the common word 'justice' in this attempt to trace, rather than expound, the *philosophy of Right*. I would like to investigate justice more deeply, contemplating all the special teachings about the science of Right in the detailed mirror presented by justice.

Justice is not manufactured by human beings, nor can human hands dismantle it. It is prior to laws made by human beings; such laws can only be expressions of justice.[3] Justice is the

[2] Cf. the preface to the *Nuovo Saggio intorno l'origine delle Idee*.

[3] Seneca defines law as: 'The rule of what is JUST and UNJUST' (*De Benef*. 4, 12); likewise, Clement of Alexandria (1 *Strom*.). The word *law* is taken in different meanings, and principally in the two indicated by St. Paul when he says: 'Gentiles who have not the law . . . are a law to themselves' (Rom 2: 14. Cf. *Conscience*, 49–71, 118–140). When he says, 'who have not the law', he is speaking of the *positive*, Mosaic law; and when he adds, 'they are a law to themselves', he indicates what is called *rational* law. *Positive* law always has some external expression: it is given or spoken in words, or promulgated in writing.

Nevertheless words, spoken or written, are not actually laws, but *signs*

essence of all laws to such an extent that St. Augustine had no hesitation in refusing to name as 'law' anything which lacked justice.[4] Nor does authority exist except as a servant of justice. Justice is the very essence of authority itself: 'Through me rulers rule.'[5]

13. The self-congratulation often present when new codes of law are established is therefore exaggerated, as far as I can see. Perfect legislation is not equivalent to bringing laws together in a single volume with regular divisions set out clearly and simply, and applying them uniformly and generally to every province and individual of a State, as though we were then dispensed from considering justice and injustice. The publication of new codes of law does not allow us to sit back and dispense with the study of rational Right.

I grant without difficulty that the formation of modern codes of law makes Roman law superfluous to the legislator — despite the mourning this will produce in weighty law libraries at the thought of possible bonfires.[6] Nevertheless *rational Right* is as

which communicate the *law* to others' intelligences. Law, therefore, stripped of all the signs by which it is communicated and promulgated, stands as a *concept* entrenched in the mind; it is an idea, a notion, expressing either the intrinsic order of being which demands respect of itself, or the will of the superior which also demands our respect. Because of this, I have elsewhere defined the formal law, stripped of every other accessory element, as 'a notion of the mind used for making a judgment about the morality of human actions, which must be guided by it.' In the same place I noted that such a definition is substantially the same as that given by authors who define the law as 'the reason for which things must be done' (Cf. *Principles of Ethics*, 1-19) [. . .].

[4] 'I cannot think that what is unjust can be law' (Bk. 1, *De lib arb.* c. 5; *De C. D.*, 19: 21). St. Thomas' teaching is the same (*S.T.*, I-II, q. 96, art. 4). The pagans themselves recognised that laws without justice are not properly speaking laws, but oppression. Cf. Plato, *Minos*, and Cicero, *Laws*, bk. 2.

[5] Fr. Suarez aptly applies this passage to the eternal law which is the very wisdom of God. He says: 'It is called human law because it was the *proximate* result of human intelligence and effort. I say *proximate* because in the beginning every human law is derived in some manner from the eternal law according to the words:

By me kings reign
and rulers decree what is just'
(Prov 8: [15]) (*De Legib.* bk. 1, c. 3: 17).

[6] The corpus of Roman law is valuable in so far as it contains a part of rational Right deduced and applied with admirable logic to circumstances.

necessary now as it was in the past. It would be ignorance to think otherwise and a public calamity to imagine that rational Right can be dismissed contemptuously.

Our own legislators did not treat the matter lightly. The Austrian civil code, generated in the heart of Germanic philosophy, wisely refers judges to natural Right[7] in doubtful cases. Consequently natural Right, the enduring and immense receptacle of all good laws, was finally recognised in our century as national law, thanks to the efforts of the man who played such a great part in the formation of the Austrian civil code, and who wrote so wisely in his *Natural, Individual Right*: 'Unless I am mistaken, the pretentious dream of a perfect code of law which will decide all cases has finally been swept away. What remains always and everywhere, therefore, as the code is the teaching of natural Right. This code, although subsidiary, is certain and decisive in contingent, legal cases.'[8]

14. But this was not the only reason why we have to fall back on natural Right. Even if a code of law could be established which foresaw all possible cases, it would last for only a brief period and be applicable to a single people. Later I shall have the opportunity of showing clearly in this work that the elements to be decided in legal cases differ from one people to another, and even amongst the same people change with the times. But whenever the universal law of justice is applied to cases, it cannot be other than itself, simple and definitive.

I would be the first, therefore, to ask for Italy what Thibaut

From this point of view the study of Roman law disciplines and directs human reason, and withholds it from the paradoxes in which ignorance and passion implicate it. This is a kind of hidden reason in favour of Roman law which serious, respectable people regard as a safeguard and teacher of jural reason. And under this aspect they are correct. But we must also look at the other side of the coin. We are dealing with a teacher whose ignorance and mistakes are extremely serious. Because of the exaggerated authority which Roman law has been granted, its errors have unfortunately been placed at the very heart of history along with the Gospel itself. And the errors would go on forever if they were to be endlessly backed by the same kind of exaggerated authority. Cf. Haller's observations on the errors arising from a false application of Roman laws in *Ristaurazione della Scienza Politica*, t. 1, c. 7: 3.

[7] §7.

[8] Zeiller, §25.

wanted for Germany,[9] that is, a common code of law for all the Italian regions. I would insist even more on a common procedure which would certainly be one of the most powerful, pacifying means — and a moral means worthy of the wisdom of rulers — for bringing together and reuniting the scattered members of our beautiful country.[10]

Such a code of law was first proposed by Caesar[11] and put into effect by Theodoric, Justinian, Frederick and Napoleon. But this was not the result of regarding such codes as instruments of power and absolute imperial authority, as some have supposed.[12] Codes of law like these are natural effects that depend for their possibility on unity of power.

15. The formation of a code of law is such an immense work that it can only be undertaken when a strong hand holds the reins of State. The formation of a code, therefore, is not a reason for denigrating monarchies. On the contrary such a code is the greatest glory of this kind of government and acknowledged today as indispensable by the good sense of the most civilised nations.[13]

We have to reprove Napoleon's anguished cry, however, which he is said to have uttered when he beheld the first commentary on his civil code: 'My code has perished.' Here, *human law* attempts sacrilegiously to usurp the *law of nature and of God* to which it dares to say: 'Depart from the face of the earth. Your throne is mine.' In this case, human laws, instead of presenting themselves as they are — a simple, *fallible, imperfect* declaration of rational law, and a sanction of revealed law —

[9] In his famous work, *Ueber die Nothwendigkeit eines allegmeinen bürgerlichen Rechts für Deutschland*, published in 1814.

[10] We should be grateful to their majesties the Emperor of Austria and the King of Sardegna who have hinted at such a worthy, useful aim in their law of copyright which effects almost the whole of Italy.

[11] Suetonius says expressly in his *Life of Caesar*: '[Caesar wished] to summarise civil law in a certain way, and produce from the immensely extended volume of laws a small number of books containing the best and most necessary laws' (C. 44).

[12] M. E. Lerminier.

[13] Romagnosi observed rightly that monarchy is the form of government most readily disposed to give peoples good civil laws. This is true of the moderate, reasonable monarchies of which we are speaking.

begin with a supremely solemn lie and injustice by offering themselves to the public as almighty, unique, infallible, unappealable, inflexible and unchangeable.

16. For myself, I would prefer to see the supreme authority preface the venerated code of social laws with the simple words: 'The only law of the State, to which we ourselves are subject, is justice as declared by reason enlightened by the Gospel. The laws which follow are expressions of that justice and have been produced by us with the greatest light which we could procure. If anything proves inexact in what we have written, we shall rectify it by using the greatest source of light at our disposition. Against the sole law of justice, our own decision or interpretation is invalid.'

Sacred, noble words like these, which express all that is most worthy in the social hierarchy and all that is most powerful and authoritative in a nation, would indicate a firm desire to maintain and protect justice by submission to it. They would do no damage whatsoever to the authority of human legislation, but rather serve as a sacred seal imposed on human legislation by God, the supreme Emperor of the universe. They would draw reverence for laws even from those who are the fiercest opponents of codes of law.

17. We should be careful to avoid thinking badly of those who feel they have to oppose codes of law. In fact, these authors possess the clearest and most far-seeing minds which are not deceived by the exterior, brief and elegant forms of laws applauded by lesser minds. The opposition to codes of law in such penetrating, acute persons is caused by the concept they have formed about codes, which they conceive as 'a certain legal programme by which the State irrevocably abolishes everything not contained in the programme.' This concept was De Savigny's starting point in his bitter attack on so-called *codification*,[14] and no one could withstand his masterly attacks as long as he held such a position.

18. The concept, however, is historical, and this is its defect. It depends on the critique of actual examples of codes of law. Needless to say, it is impossible to argue with De Savigny's

[14] The famous dissertation, *Our century's calling to contribute to legislation and jurisprudence*, was his answer to Thibaut's work (cf. ftn. 8).

position if a code is offered to the people as a divine oracle demanding worship of its dispositions, or set out once and for all as though it were the eternal, immutable law of God. No one can deny that the formation of codes of law means death to science, a life of ignorance, the rule of mediocrity, the exile of genius, the destruction of national customs, rejection of traditions, the oppression of freedom, the degradation of justice and the blocking of humanity in its journey towards progress. Certainly, I have no intention whatsoever of denying this. From this point of view, I feel myself completely at one with the standard-bearer of the historical school.

But I have to differ when he speaks of the kind of code of law that we shall have in the future. What is required is a code which prescribes *justice*, and is not itself an injustice. We need a code whose first words are indicative of HUMILITY, the foundation and principle of all human justice. I am well aware that this will be scorned by some philosophers, but we must remember, despite the mockery, that humility is a public virtue, not simply a private affair as some people believe; it is above all a public, regal virtue. In other words, if we are to have a code which can validly subject human beings to its own rule, it must be subject to God. Our business as human beings is not to make laws but, as we have said, to interpret carefully the *supreme jural law* by means of all the enlightenment available to us. This interpretation will always be modifiable, but not as the result of caprice. It will not be found where power is greatest, but where the greatest wisdom is used by legislative authority. And the interpretation will remain constant and unchanged until this wisdom decrees otherwise.

19. In classical times, it was proverbial that *judges* should be ruled by *laws*, and *people* by judges.[15] Living as we do in the light of the gospel, we have to add that '*laws* themselves must be ruled by *eternal justice*'. In other words, positive law must be subject to rational law, which must always be able to be heard; positive law must also be declared on every occasion according to the best available reason which has to ponder all the

[15] 'As the laws rule the judges, so the magistrates rule the people. It can be said that the magistrate is the law as spoken, and the law the silent magistrate' (Cicero, *Laws*, 3: 1; he follows Plato, *Laws*, 4).

circumstances as well as the natural and supernatural data. This greatest of all rational authority[16] must always have free voice in the State, and act as living legislation which corrects written, dead legislation. Every authority must take its stand only on what is good and true, not on what is evil and false. As St. Paul said in those divine words: 'For we cannot do anything against the truth, but only for the truth.'[17]

The *philosophy of Right*, therefore, considered as the science of justice, stands as the unshaken foundation of every human authority and of every legislation which springs from such authority; this explains its supreme importance.

20. Other reflections serve to increase even more the importance of the philosophy of Right.

Jurisprudence can be considered as a *science* or as an *art*. We have already spoken about it as *science*. But what would it be as *art* if it abandoned the light of rational Right and deserted justice as an end, in order to keep solely to the material letter of the law and aim at settling cases abstractly, without reference to their justice or injustice? Common sense provides an immediate answer for everyone with good sense. Distressed families and all nations, which pay in various ways for such an attitude, also know the answer.

Abstractions of this kind are absurd because they endeavour to consider the matter in hand without reference to its *essence*, while retaining only its accidents; the art of jurisprudence, which is *essentially* the art of bringing about the triumph of justice, is carried out as though justice did not exist for it. We are no longer dealing with jurisprudence now, but with some other art which retains the old name in order to deceive people. It could be called 'the art of winning just and unjust cases', or the

[16] We shall show elsewhere what kind of reason must constitute the greatest natural authority of the State. Here it is sufficient to note that it would not be the greatest possible reason if it were not free of passion and cleansed from vice. Love of justice, probity and virtue are light that must be added to the light of the understanding if intelligence is not to be lost in darkness and suffocate in human stench.

[17] And almost immediately after: 'In my use of the authority which the Lord has given me for building up and not for tearing down' (2 Cor 13: [8, 10]). This great principle is the source of the sweetness, unending reasonableness and rightful flexibility of the laws of the Church.

art of deception. It might even take on some more delicate name. But it is not the art of jurisprudence, which is essentially noble because its aim is justice, the most noble of all things. What used to be the art of jurisprudence has been transformed into a vile art that is totally indifferent to either the triumph or defeat of justice and which, as such, is proper to the devil himself, although practised by human beings.

Cipolla, Ferrario and others, with their detestable treatises *De Cautelis*, are tolerated by our foolish world, and even considered great, practical legal experts.[18] What a state mankind finds itself in! The science of justice, the philosophy of Right, throws its light upon such practices as these, and clearly shows their distastefulness and cruelty. The public, enlightened in this way, will no longer tolerate such open wickedness.

II.

The distinction between the philosophy of right and related sciences

21. The philosophy of Right is that which gives life to *positive laws* and to the *art* of jurisprudence. This is sufficient to indicate its importance. But before examining the philosophy of Right, we need to define it and sketch its outline by distinguishing it carefully from sciences connected with it. This will ensure first that our discussion is confined within necessary limits, and

[18] One of Cipolla's cautions states: 'A caution for one who owes a large sum: pay a little in the hope of being freed from the obligation.' The great jurist praises this advice: 'I will give one admirable caution which you must always remember.' One of Tommaso Ferrario's cautions is intended to ensure that a beneficed person does not lose his benefice even if he has committed murder: 'A caution against a prelate's losing his benefices because he has committed murder.' Another of his cautions is about speaking badly of another with impunity: 'A caution for avoiding a harmful legal action when using harmful words against another.' For arguments against the use made of *cautions* by these authors, and against petty lawyers who employ other morally wrong artifices: cf. Samuel Stryck, *De Cautelis contractuum*, sect. 1, c. 1 (Wittenberg, 1690) and Kaspar Ziegler, *Rabulistica* (Dresden, 1685).

second that it is carried forward within those limits in an orderly, clear and scientific fashion. We have to ask what the philosophy of Right is, what its related sciences are, and how it is distinguished from them.

The *philosophy of Right* is the *doctrine of first reasons applied to jural justice*. And *jural justice* is justice rooted in rights.

The sciences connected with the philosophy of Right are principally positive Jurisprudence; the philosophy of positive Right; natural or rational Right; politics, and especially morals, and eudaimonology.

We have already seen how the *philosophy of Right* is superior to *positive jurisprudence*. The former lawfully generates the latter; the latter is generated from the former just as consequences are generated from principles, which implicitly contain all consequences. The philosophy of Right is the reason and authority behind positive jurisprudence which it also emends, tutors and interprets. This was admirably clear to the greatest minds of antiquity who were happy to pass from the narrow study of limited civil law to the wider fields of jural philosophy. Plato and Cicero are examples who spring to mind immediately.

22. Let me quote from Cicero's book on laws, which he puts in the form of a dialogue between himself, his brother Quintus and their friend Atticus. His fertile words show how the great minds of antiquity were clearly aware of the superiority of the philosophy of Right over legal minutiae.

We can also see from these words the kind of research they undertook, and how impossible it is for a person of great intelligence to consider the arid details of positive decisions without reaching out in spirit to the universal reason and foundations that sustain such decisions. Plato is used as an example in these words of Cicero. And this is what Cicero tells his friend, T. Pomponius, when the latter asks what he thinks about civil law:

> *Cicero*. Remember that the greatest men in our city used to interpret it to the people, and answer questions about it. Although they were taken up with matters of great importance, they were also engaged in minute affairs. What is so great as the common right, and so minute, yet so necessary to the people, as the office of these consultants? I do not think for a moment that those responsible for such an

office were ignorant of universal right. But they exercised what they call civil right because their only wish was to dominate the people.[19] Universal right was set aside as less necessary for ordinary use.

So what are you asking me? Are you encouraging me to compile booklets about rights connected with water collection or boundary walls, or to record contractual formulas and judicial decisions? These things have already been dealt with carefully and at length by many authors. Besides they are too insignificant for me to expect you to be interested in them.

Atticus. Look, this is what I am interested in. You have written about the perfect state of the republic, and it would seem obvious that you should now continue to write about laws. Your Plato did the same, I see, and you admire him above all others.

Marcus. Remember how, on a summer's day, Plato discussed with Clinia, the Cretan, and Megillo, the Spartan, the constitutions of republics and their wonderful laws. The three of them walked and sat amongst the cypresses and woods of Gnossus, and we can do the same, discussing the things they discussed while we walk and rest amidst these tall poplars in the shade of these steep green banks. It will certainly be more fruitful than talking about what happens in the forum.

Atticus. These are the things I want to talk about.

Marcus. Well, Quintus, what about it?

Quintus. There could be nothing better.

Marcus. You're right. Remember that this is the very best kind of argument for showing beautifully what human beings have been given by nature, how many SUPREMELY GOOD THINGS the human mind contains, what responsibilities we are born to cultivate and exercise. When we uncover these things, we already find ourselves at the source of laws and right.

Atticus. So you do not think that the subject of Right

[19] *Hoc (ius) civile quod vocant eatenus exercuerunt, quoad populum praestare voluerunt*. These words, if my interpretation is not mistaken, would seem to confirm the opinion of modern writers who regard the *solemn formulas*, to which ancient Roman jurisprudence attributed so much importance, as a political tool of the aristocracy. By means of these formulas, the aristocracy gained a monopoly of the science of Right and thus held the people dependent upon them for decisions when judgment had to be given.

should be sought from praetorian edicts, as many imagine nowadays, nor from the XII Tables, as our ancestors thought, but sought from the depths of philosophy?
Marcus. Yes! And the reason, Pomponius, is that we are not researching legal cautions[20] or the replies sought in the course of consultations. These are not light matters, of course, and it is good that they should have been investigated by great men in the past, and in the present by the one who holds supreme authority and wisdom. But in our discussion we should embrace the entire cause of universal rights and of laws in such a way that what we call civil right may be restricted within the small and narrow sphere of nature. We have to declare the nature of right, and seek it in the nature of human beings. We have to think about the laws which are suitable for governing communities, and then discuss the rights and statutes of civilised peoples in which the rights of our own people are included.
Quintus. You're right to begin at this high level, my friend. It really is necessary to start at the beginning. Anyone who begins to teach civil right from some other starting point is not dealing with the ways of justice, but with litigation.

23. This quotation shows that the distinction between the *philosophy of Right* and *positive Right* was recognised very early. Greek and Roman sages themselves realised that the latter without the former was simply degenerate, ruinous litigation rather than the art of making justice prevail in human society. The quotation also shows that positive, lowly, detailed right, which of itself is contemptible, acquires its greatness, dignity, decency and entire utility from philosophy. It shows also that it is the duty of the philosophy of Right to lead laws back to their primitive source from which this philosophy then has to unleash the just sanctions which alone must preside over the nations and which alone can help them. The philosophy of Right rejects, as spurious and illegitimate, sanctions which are not generated and contained virtually in this supreme source. Its duty is also to penetrate human nature and discover those *supremely good things*, inserted by nature in the human mind,

[20] *Quemadmodum caveamus in jure.*

which underlie the force of every right and the strength of every obligation.[21]

24. The science of *natural Right* and the *philosophy of positive Right* are as it were two parts of the *universal philosophy of Right*. The science of natural right studies the *principle of rights* and from it deduces particular rights, some of which belong to human beings by nature, some of which are consequences of particular natural rights. In the same way, the *philosophy of positive Right* first studies how positive laws should be made. Then it considers the laws of the State, confronting them with the ideal laws which it has formulated in order to test the civil laws and see if they are justly directed to the protection of true rights. In other words, the laws of the State have to protect true rights exactly, neither more nor less. They are not to invade natural freedom and thus violate rather than maintain the rights of individuals nor are they to create new, arbitrary and imaginary rights, nor overlook any rights which could and should be forcefully protected.

It is clear therefore that the *universal philosophy of Right* has three responsibilities. It first establishes what human rights there are, then how positive legislation should be brought about, and finally undertakes a critique of positive laws. Such a critique can only be undertaken successfully when it is known which positive laws have to be made, and how they are to be made. There are therefore three fundamental jural sciences:

1. That which determines the nature of *rights* — *rational Right*;

2. That which applies rational Right to possible positive laws and shows how these laws should be made — the *theory of positive laws*;

3. That which applies the theory of positive laws to real positive laws in different States and indicates their advantages and defects — the *critique of positive laws*.

25. The last two sciences are together called the *philosophy of positive laws* which is a union of sciences rather than a single science.[22]

[21] *Quid sit homini tributum natura, quantum* VIM RERUM OPTIMARUM *mens humana contineat.*

[22] Lampredi erred, as Signor Baroli justly noted, when he defined natural

It is clear that the third science, the *critique of positive laws* is never-ending because it expands and divides in a way similar to that of the various laws and legislations which have ruled the various peoples of the earth in different times and places. For my part, I have preferred to call this book *The Philosophy of Right* precisely because such a title expresses the result of an admixture of all the three named sciences.

I did indeed begin with the simple intention of expounding the principles of rational Right. But as I wrote, I realised that the teachings relative to rational Right were clarified to a great extent by applying them now and again to existing civil legislations, and vice versa. *Historical method* is thus intermingled with *rational method*.[23] This is, I think, the most secure and

Right as *the critique of laws which have to be made, and the study of laws which have been made.* This is the definition of the *philosophy of positive Right.* And even Kant, who devoted himself to indicating the precise boundaries between one science and another, seems not to have presented the true, correct definition of *rational Right* when he defined it as 'the complex of conditions in which external legislation is possible'. This definition simply indicates a *relationship* between *rational Right* and *external legislation.* But the relationships between one thing and another are never the essential element of the thing under consideration. Seeking the nature of *rational Right* is one matter; seeking its relationship with external legislation is another. According to us rational Right is 'the science that determines rights'. Its relationship with civil legislation consists principally in this: 'The rights determined by the science of rational Right become the object of external legislation in so far as the latter expresses and sanctions the former.'

Kant's definition, however, is coherent with his principle of 'co-existence'. For him, rights arise from the necessity of social co-existence. This in turn is the effect and the condition determined by *external legislation*, and must therefore be determined through the scientific development of rights. There are no rights in Kant's system other than those constituting the *conditions* which make *external legislation*, and therefore *society* and human co-existence, possible. We shall examine this kind of system in its own place. — Cf. my *Storia comparativa de' sistemi morali*, c. 5, a. 11 and 12.

[23] I have indicated the advantages of this historico-rational method (which is my normal way of procedure,) in the *Introduction* to the *Anthropology* [*Anthropology as an Aid to Moral Science*]. On the one hand, therefore, I am glad to agree with the German philosophers when they maintain that the historical element does not enter *science*, which is completely speculative. On the other hand, I cannot grant the consequence which some of them draw from this truth, that is, that history is useless to science. History provides the mind with data and authorities. In its turn, authority is extremely helpful to

persuasive way of making progress. It is also of more practical use in so far as the application of theory is foreseen and indicated beforehand. Nevertheless, the principal part of this work concerns rational Right.

26. But what is the relationship between the *philosophy of Right* and the *philosophy of politics*? I have already described the nature and division of the philosophy of politics elsewhere, and I assume that the reader is aware of what I have written.[24] I listed four kinds of *political criteria*, the second of which contains the criteria drawn from the examination of the *natural construction of civil society*.[25] Justice is the first element to enter the construction of every human society. In the last analysis, a society cannot be anything except an accumulation of rights and duties. Society is a complex of agreements, which themselves are acts of justice. There can in fact be no agreement at all except between people who maintain and make others believe that they wish to stand loyally by the word they have given. Society itself is an effect or work of justice which exercises its authority over mankind.[26]

The theory of justice, therefore, is a part of the theory of society. Vice versa, the theory of society is, under another aspect, part of the theory of justice. Consequently, the politician, that is, the person who is responsible for governing society, must be aware before all else of the theory of justice. He should be especially mindful of that part of justice which binds individuals and joins them in society (this part is normally called *internal public Right*). Unless practical politics aims at conserving the bonds with which justice draws together the various members of society, it will soon become clear that such politics cannot succeed in developing society nor even in holding it together.

The preservation of social rights is, therefore, identical with the preservation of society. If the first duty of politics is to preserve society,[27] its first duty is also to defend the social rights

the understanding in finding the path which leads it safely to the speculative truths for which it is searching.

[24] In the *Prefazione alle opere politiche* [. . .].

[25] *Ibid*., p. 21; and *Society and its Purpose*, *Introduction*.

[26] This was demonstrated more fully in *SP*, bk. 1, c. 2.

[27] It is self-evident that the preservation of the existence of society is the

that form and constitute society. These rights are the cement that binds society together. The *philosophy of Right*, therefore, as the science of *social justice*, is the *end* relative to the *philosophy of politics*; and the *philosophy of politics* is the means relative to the *philosophy of Right*. We obtain the same result if we compare *politics* with the other part of the *theory of justice*, which concerns the rights of individuals and is commonly called *private Right* or, as I call it, *individual Right*.

27. The preservation of the rights of individuals is a part of their *moral good* and of their *eudaimonological good*. Moral good requires that a person respect the rights of others; eudaimonological good requires that the same person's rights be respected by others. But if what I have said about the nature of the science and the art of government in civil, communal groups is true — that is, government is simply 'a means of obtaining and increasing the good and perfection of the individuals who make up the social body'[28] — it follows that politics can exist only on condition that it first keeps in view all the rights that individuals possess. These rights form the end of government. If government has to promote the moral good, it must consequently *persuade* all those who are governed to respect the rights of others; if government has to promote the eudaimonological good, it must defend with *force* all the rights of every person who is governed so that no one will dare violate them. These are the two great duties of governments. Government, therefore, must not simply use force, but also every means of reasonable persuasion. With force alone, it can only weakly and partially maintain the eudaimonological good of individuals. Force can never promote moral good which depends on the spontaneous movement of disciplined and well-disposed wills. And it is clear that human perfection, which always resides in individuals, and is the end of politics, consists in both categories of good, *moral* and *eudaimonological*.

28. Hence the *philosophy of politics* followed the *philosophy of*

first, and the most important duty of the science and art of politics. Nevertheless, governments sometimes lose sight of their responsibility in order to attain some apparent good. This accounts for the decline of civil societies, as I have shown in *SC*.

[28] Cf. *PE*, 9 ss.

Right, just as a science concerned with means takes its order and direction from a science concerned with ends. Moreover, anyone who has not clearly understood a science concerned with ends cannot usefully be taught anything about a science of means. The reader will therefore see immediately why in this series I have begun with the moral and jural works and then moved on to political studies. He will also see how absurd and wrong it is to consider political doctrine in abstraction from jural teaching, as Machiavelli did (and he was the first amongst many). Politics cannot go its own way, cut off from jural teaching whose humble servant it is. It is impossible to conceive of the prosperity of a society of rational, moral beings (and this is the aim of politics) without simultaneously conceiving the development and increasing perfection of reason and morality which constitute and inform that society.

29. Finally we have to compare the science of Right with *eudaimonology* and with *ethics*, establishing its limits relative to them in such a way that all three are confined to their own territory without impinging on that of the others. We need to know, therefore, whether Right[29] is a part of ethics, or ethics treated under some other aspect, as has sometimes been thought, or whether Right is perhaps a kind of branch of eudaimonology.

My own view is that the science of Right stands between eudaimonology and ethics in such a way that its two extremes each touch one of these other sciences. Let me explain.

I understand the word 'right' as 'a faculty which human beings have for doing or experiencing[30] anything useful. It is protected by the moral law which obliges others to respect this faculty.' But the faculty for doing or experiencing anything useful to human beings is a eudaimonological good. In this sense rights pertain properly speaking to eudaimonology. An evident proof of this is found in the fact that a person with more right than another is said to be more fortunate, not morally better.

On the other hand, right is not simply a mere eudaimonological faculty. The faculty could never be called 'right' unless it

[29] 'Right' spelt with a capital letter stands for 'the science of rights'.

[30] The word 'experience' expresses in its general and philosophical sense every kind of passivity, even a pleasurable kind.

were protected and defended by the moral law which prohibits all other human beings, or some of them, from attacking it. Consequently, the protection afforded by the moral law is properly speaking the *form* by which the merely *eudaimonological* by nature takes on *jural* dignity.

The science of Right, therefore, has *eudaimonological good* as its matter to the extent that what is good in this respect is regulated and protected by the moral law. It is properly speaking a science concerned with the *relationship* between what is eudaimonological and what is moral.

30. It should be easy now to understand how our way of conceiving Right places it as a science between *eudaimonology* and *ethics*, although fully distinct from both of them. It is also clear that Right has been wrongly defined by some as 'the science of jural laws'. In fact, these laws, which are a class of moral laws,[31] do nothing more than impress a seal on the faculty, enhancing it so that it possesses the moral uprightness enabling it to be called 'a right'. Nevertheless, this faculty of doing and experiencing, enhanced in this way, always remains the proper subject of the science of Right. The law that enhances the faculty is never the subject of the science of Right.

III.

History of the science of natural Right

31. These distinctions between the *philosophy of Right* and its connected, bordering sciences enable us to set the boundaries which have to govern our study and facilitate order and scientific method in dealing with this branch of philosophy. It is clear

[31] I cannot agree with Kant who completely separates *jural* from *ethical duties*, although I do maintain that 'merely ethical duties' are excluded from jural duties. The motion of *duty* would cease entirely if it did not include some moral obligation. For me, every duty is essentially ethical.

that *scientific* treatment of a subject requires constant adherence to a thread of reasoning which springs from a single, extremely simple principle; *scientific* treatment is not free (as *common* or *familiar* treatment are) to step aside a little from the subject under consideration. But in order to work in this way, we first have to define clearly what we are dealing with, and the limits within which it is contained. We cannot say that a science exists if our treatment of the matter in hand is not carried out with exact, controlled logic.

It follows that the history of various doctrines considered as sciences is reduced to the history of the more or less precise forms and refined methods with which these sciences have been carried out over the years. In every discipline we have to distinguish carefully between the *history of science* and the *history of opinion*, the two kinds of history.

32. My understanding of *science* is: 'a system of truths dependent upon a single principle'; my understanding of *opinion* is: 'everything that people have known or thought or simply believed'. It is clear, of course, that opinion or simple knowledge of things was present in the world long before the invention of sciences understood in the strict meaning of the word. It is also clear, because cognition and opinion pertain to mankind while sciences are proper to a few individuals, that the history of an opinion in any subject must be referred back to a period considerably antedating the history of the science corresponding to that opinion. The history of opinion is coeval with mankind, and can be assembled from languages, symbols, monuments, customs and chronicles; the history of science begins with the first scientists and is found principally in their individual writings.

33. Applying this distinction to the *history of Right*, we cannot doubt that human beings knew both *right* and *obligation* from the first moment of their existence on earth. Long before Plato and Pythagoras, human beings were taught, especially by their ancient traditions, what would later be written down so well in Italy and Greece. Peoples learned from their own traditions how to educate their reasoning and their noble feeling.

Even those determined to write down what mankind had known for so long prior to their own time worked according to the method they had learned from the people, their great common master. Although these writers were capable of reflection, of ordering, deducing and linking together the homogeneous parts of common knowledge, of presenting their work in logical form, and enhancing it with a kind of divine eloquence that seemed to bring new light to those who marvelled at what had been accomplished, they were unable and unwilling to reduce their work to the strict forms of discipline which would render it 'science', as we would now call it. The first authors were extremely intelligent, highly motivated and quite different from their contemporaries, but this did not distant them from the familiar, flexible way of reasoning they had inherited.

34. In fact, progress requires that the great work of collating the teachings of mankind (of which we are now speaking) and forming them into sciences, should proceed according to the following steps: first, the doctrines must be collected and summarised in pithy phrases; then they have to be expressed in poetry and clothed in fine images. Without this, society, the people as a whole, cannot savour and penetrate the dignity and sublimity of the message coming to them through the medium of symbols, living images and figures. If society were not drawn to feel the importance and beauty of such written doctrines, the content of the books would never occupy people's attention. No one ever began to write something original without the precious hope that his unique contribution to literature would be read widely.

35. At this point, more penetrating minds begin to pay attention to the rational part of what has been written. They devote their attention to what seems slight, specialised and almost buried under the weight of literary embellishment, but which they realise is the firm foundation of everything else. Having experienced what lies beyond the images that cover it, they never abandon what they have come to appreciate. The underlying truth becomes the sole object of their concern and love, and they undertake a new method of work quite opposite to that of their predecessors. In other words, they now start to strip the doctrine of the trappings in which it had first been clothed and enfolded.

36. During this period, the logical minds of the learned begin the great labour entailed in working through naked, but disconnected doctrines in order to bring together under a single head

the scattered parts for which human intelligences are searching. Up to this moment there is no division between sciences. The whole of human knowledge, still divided into particular pieces of information mixed up together, stands before the researcher. Each of the numerous particles of information haphazardly drawn together requires mental attention or verbal expression. A long, slow labour is then protracted over centuries during which the clever people most interested in cognition diligently separate different pieces of knowledge which they later collect into various stacks, as it were.

37. New generations of enquirers come along and note with joy the gradual accumulation of these stacks of knowledge from which they begin to fashion orderly buildings according to thought-out designs of varying beauty. But these first edifices of science are not altogether successful for several reasons. First, the materials necessary for regularity and fine finish have not all been discovered, nor worked upon in such a way that they can be put together accurately. The designs used depend more on the available materials than upon what is needed for the building itself. Moreover, the materials themselves have not all been accurately classified and separated; some are mistakenly placed in stacks to which they do not belong. Thirdly, the novice-architects must necessarily form their vision of the work as they go along, and will inevitably fail in merging satisfactorily the various stones they possess. These and other causes ensure that the first attempt at reducing disconnected information to a scientific form results in irregular, incomplete constructions, lacking the truth and elegance which is aimed at, and which will one day be achieved. The last and most difficult operation is to build a science entirely of its own materials, without borrowing from other sciences, so that it stands on its own, although in continuity with other sciences from which it is carefully separated.

Considerations of this kind show that in the history of a science as such, we have to describe all the successive operations undertaken by the learned to reduce the subject to the form of a science. It is indeed very difficult if not impossible to assign the precise point at which one of these operations begins and the other ends. Nevertheless in attempting this, it is better to be satisfied with maintaining a firm, ordered series of ideas than insisting on temporal succession. Over-attention to fixed dates sometimes produces the opposite effect from that intended, with the result that historical facts are forced and distorted for the sake of compressing them into periods where they do not fit.

38. Hufeland's[32] *History of the science of Right*, although an admirable and much imitated attempt at distinguishing various periods in the history of this science, fails because it attempts to record exactly the times in which these periods fall. In the book, Hufeland first distinguishes three periods in the history of Right and describes them excellently as periods of *fragmentary* treatment, *systematic-indeterminate* treatment, and *systematic-determinate* treatment. But attempts by historians to establish more precisely the periods in which one division ends and another begins are clearly forced and false.

For some, the second period starts with Grotius[33] and the third with Christian Wolff.[34] It is true that the works of Grotius and Wolfe are the weightiest that have been written on the subject, and do indeed mark an epoch. But if we wish to indicate the epochs of a science by following the development of ideas (which rise to new levels in certain periods) rather than the fame in which books are held, we find that the works of these two men certainly cannot serve as signs that human understanding has begun a new journey. An accurate history of the science of Right would have to distinguish the *development of ideas amongst the learned* from the development of the *book-form* to which these ideas are consigned. When these two developments have been distinguished, the three periods we have mentioned can be seen in each of them, and can be outlined as follows:

Period 1. The period of *fragmentary treatment*, when writers, although dealing with rights and obligations as occasion offers or in passing, do not give them exclusive, reflective

[32] Cf. his *Sistema del Diritto naturale*, Jena, 1765, and *Saggio sui principi del Diritto naturale*.

[33] 1625 is the date of the first Paris edition of his *De jure belli et pacis*.

[34] The first edition of his *Jus naturae* is dated 1740. Others make the third period begin with Christian Thomasius's *Fundamenta juris nat. et gentium*, Halle, 1705.

attention, nor separate them from other notions. On the contrary, they mix them with other ideas which they force them to serve.

Period 2. The period of *systematic-indeterminate treatment*, when writers begin to fix their attention on rights which they coerce into a system by working to purify them of every heterogeneous element (that is, of elements which belong to other sciences).

Period 3. The period of *systematic-determinate treatment*, when the learned have succeeded in entirely separating the science of Right from all other sciences near or bordering upon it, in determining its sphere, and in defining its matter accurately. This final period still has room, however, for developing what has been well-defined and separated, and penetrating it more deeply.

39. Such a triple work can obviously be carried out upon ideas before it is expressed in books, and this, I think, is what took place in the two periods long before Grotius and Wolff. Could we find, for example, more balanced ideas about natural Right than those in the *Summa* of St. Thomas Aquinas?[35] These ideas, besides being logically interconnected, coherent and resplendent, are also deduced from a single principle. In other words, they contain everything needed to make them a science. Before Grotius, many ecclesiastical writers, following St. Thomas, wrote treatises *de justitia et jure*, and accurately discussed the doctrines of natural Right. Lessius and De Lugo are good examples. The *development of ideas* exists, therefore, and the work of the first two periods had already been done before Grotius' time. However, these ideas had not been included in a separate book. What was lacking was simply their *book-form* — that is, the art of making books from these ideas. Nothing was missing from their status as science. This is a consideration totally disregarded by our historians of the science.

Moreover, if the passage from the period of *fragmentary treatment* to that of *systematic-indeterminate treatment* is marked by the form and title of books, it has to be dated some time before Grotius, whose own book deals only with part, not the

[35] In II-II, q. 57–120. Even these ideas are in part deduced from preceding writers going back as far as Aristotle.

whole of Right.[36] Its title shows that it is not concerned with a complete science. We have to go back to Oldendorp,[37] Hemming,[38] Stefano,[39] Gentile,[40] and even further.

40. An unbiased and impartial historian of the science of Right will also have to note accurately that there were two professions, theologians and jurists, amongst the first writers on the subject. He will also discover without difficulty that the *development of ideas* about natural Right was far superior amongst theologians than amongst jurists. My own opinion is that none of the great principles of natural Right was lacking in the ecclesiastical writers of the 4th century, when St. Augustine lived. I say 'writers' because minds were certainly not devoid of these principles after the preaching of the Gospel. The jurists, however, furthered the *development* of the exterior *form* (what I have called *book-form*). The reason for this is clear.

Jurists needed to discover the reasons upholding positive Right, which alone could justify and explain positive law, and correct what might be lacking in it. When united, the reasons behind positive right constitute *rational Right*. They were however ignored or barely touched upon in positive Right as a result of the prejudice (I was tempted to say the eternal prejudice) which drives legislators to make laws depend upon authority, not on clear reason.[41] Jurists realised that they had to make up for this defect in positive decisions by investigating separately the dictates of natural reason, from which human positive laws draw their entire usefulness and true authority. In fact, the first treatises on *rational Right* were published only under the form of an *Introduction to Roman law*.[42]

Theologians were not under the same kind of pressure. In

36 Grotius deals directly only with the 'right of nations'.

37 Jo. Oldendorp, *Isagoge, seu elementa introd. jur. nat. gent. et civ.* Col. Agripp., 1539.

38 Nic. Hemming, *De leg. nat. methodo apodict*, Vit., 1564.

39 Matt. Stefano, *Method. tract. de arte juris*, Gryisw., 1615.

40 Alberico Gentile, born 1551 in Castel San Gennasio, in the Marche d'Ancona, wrote a number of books, among them *De jure belli, libri tres*. Hanau., 1598, in 8.

41 Thomasius elevated this principle to the level of a maxim.

42 They were, according to the barbarous, but effective expression of Senkenberg, a *Jus civile naturalisatum* [civil law naturalised].

Christian theology they already possessed the doctrines of rational Right (and many others) and the roots of canonical right. They did not have to investigate these doctrines separately, outside theology, as jurists had to investigate them outside certain laws, and as an aid to these laws. It is true that in theology itself theologians found it convenient to separate the part which expounds the truths which have to be believed (which they called *dogmatic* theology) from the part which expounds the truths which have to direct actions (which they called *moral* theology). But they left the jural doctrines, which they always considered relative to morals (that is, in so far as they helped human beings to govern themselves and work for moral good), mixed with morals. This explains why theologians went no further with the methodical separation of Right from morals, a division which is almost wholly due to jurists, and later to philosophers.

41. Let us take as an example the year 1740, in which Christian Wolff published his *Jus naturae*, and ask ourselves if it is the best date for establishing the third-period epoch, that is, the period of *systematic-determinate treatment*. Examining the question we shall see immediately that the facts have been mishandled for the sake of subjecting them to an overpowering, preconceived order.

Delaying the start of the second-period epoch to 1625, the year of publication of *De jure belli et pacis*, is, I think, a mistake. On the other hand, the third-period epoch, if indeed it is an epoch, is made to start too soon. This epoch is one in which Right is treated entirely on its own, cut off and divided from every other science. But the work entailed in separating and dividing the doctrine of natural Right from that of every other science, and from ethics in particular, takes place in the second period; it was not completed either with Thomasius or with Wolff. The authors who followed Wolff were all strenuously engaged in this work, often without agreement amongst themselves. Even Kant was unable to draw a line between the sciences in a way that satisfied everybody.

42. The reason prompting the historians of rational Right to think that this science had been perfectly separated from all others in the works of Thomasius, Grundling, Gherardo and Wolff is its separation, in the external form of their treatises, of the science of Right from moral science. The development of

form proceeded more quickly than the development of *ideas*. Although these authors fully intended to separate the sciences from the point of view of ideas also, they offered nothing more than promises to this effect. It is external forms and promises (which do indeed allow us to know the authors' views) that attract the attention of those who write the literary history of sciences.[43]

43. If all these writers had together succeeded in drawing the correct line between natural Right and the other sciences, especially ethics, as they had proposed and promised, it would not have been necessary for Zeiller, a famous German, to have written:

> The whole merit of critical philosophy lies in having identified certain definite signs that distinguish jurisprudence from neighbouring sciences, in having accurately determined the principal ideas which up till now have remained uncertain, in having introduced into jurisprudence the formal principles taken from the form of pure reason, and in having thus elevated jurisprudence to the status of a science.[44]

It is Zeiller's opinion, therefore, that before Kant the concept of Right had not been fully distinguished from that of morals. But we may go on to ask whether this work was then completed by Kant himself or by his followers. Zeiller adds immediately:

> Nevertheless, the philosophers of law, who held to a formal principle, were once more divided in their opinions. The particular difficulty was that some admit a principle of right independent of the supreme law of virtue, and some think that the principle of right has to depend in part absolutely and in part relatively on the principle of ethics.[45]

It is clear, therefore, that the relationships between Right and

[43] Another defect that can generally be observed in those who undertake to write 'literary histories' is that they do not distinguish 'the history of the science', which consists in describing the development of ideas (the most difficult and profound part of their work) from the 'history of the influence exercised by authors on the development of the science itself.'

[44] Zeiller, *Diritto privato*, 37.

[45] *Ibid.*

ethics were still not fixed to the satisfaction of all the interested parties. It cannot be said that the concept of Right and that of ethics were so clearly established that they were utterly distinct; nor can it be said therefore that the third period of *systematic-determinate* treatment had truly begun. For this to happen, the concept of Right would have to be fully determined and detached from all other concepts. The work of this third period is to bring Right to perfection after it has previously been distinguished from all other sciences.

44. We can understand better the imperfection remaining even now in the science of Right if we expound briefly the characteristics assigned to it up to the present as criteria for distinguishing it from ethics especially.

Christian Thomasius was not content to recognise as jural only negative obligations, although such obligations are jural as we shall show. He also wanted to separate Right from ethics in such a way that Right would be concerned with the *external action* alone, and ethics with the entire *internal* part.

This, however, does not provide the kind of simple separation of the concept of Right from that of morals which I would require in good methodological separation. What we are offered by Thomasius is a real, and therefore absurd separation. External actions cut off from intentions and internal ends are actions without dignity precisely because they are deprived of that moral and personal character which gives rise to all the respect due to human actions. There can be no *right* in a merely external action which is simply a *fact* and as such depends for its efficacy on its power. Face to face with a stronger power capable of destroying it, this fact loses its efficacy.

45. Nevertheless, the absurd division of Right from morals gained some favour during and after Thomasius's lifetime. Even Kant, the founder of the school of critical philosophy, was not exempt from this defect. He defines external legislation as: 'that which provides a motive from outside the law for observing the law'. In other words, the 'motive' is that of chastisement and punishment, which are not moral motives at all. He goes on to define Right as: 'the complex of conditions which make external legislation possible' — that is, those conditions which make possible the institution of punishment and reward for those breaking or observing the law. This shows clearly that Kant

himself considers 'Right' more or less as Thomasius does, and totally separates it from internal, moral motives of action. There is no doubt that Right, separated by such an expedient from morals, is completely cut off from morals, from which it no longer receives life. This kind of Right is totally unworthy of the name. All that remains is the carcass of Right, equivalent, as Hugo said, 'to a moral science for murderers'.[46]

Sciences must certainly be methodologically divided from one another, but they are not to lose their natural communication. If they do, they all perish. Their life comes from their connection with the whole of knowledge, just as the life of our bodily members comes from their connection with the whole body. Perhaps it will be helpful if we can see the genesis of such an error, common to almost all German authors on Right from Thomasius to Kant.

46. These writers noticed that the external legislator is unable to observe the intentions of the spirit. Moreover, rational Right was conceived by them as a guide to the legislator in his formation of civil laws. They concluded that the science of Right was to be restricted 'to the external conditions which make civil legislation possible.' But this is too hasty a conclusion. Although it is true that simply internal intentions cannot be observed by legislators and judges, it does not follow that intentions should be excluded. Rather they should be considered upright until external signs show the contrary.

Intentions are sometimes manifested externally either through words or some other kind of sign. In these cases, the legislator must take the words and other external signs as indicative of internal affections. If these signs were of no use for external legislation, the legislator would never consider what is external as indicative of what is internal. This would lead, however, to all kinds of absurdities: words themselves would have no meaning in the sight of the law. What kind of legislation would result from the abandonment of language and of every sign manifesting the interior of the spirit? But whether intentions are held to be upright when nothing is seen to the contrary from outside, or whether intentions are positively

[46] *Eine Todtsschlagsmoral.*

acknowledged for what they are and shown to be such on the basis of external signs, it still remains that external actions have a value only in reference to intentions through which alone they merit respect and the protection of the law. If moral dignity is removed from actions, they neither could nor should be the object of any legislation whatsoever.

47. We may perhaps find another reason explaining the origin of the error under consideration if we deign to open a book written about five centuries before Kant. It was always believed, as we know, that the word 'just', as a substantive ('that which is just'), expresses a quality of action, and is used without reference to the spirit of the person who does the action. St. Thomas agrees; he finds this concept in the etymology itself of the word.

> When we use the word 'just' about what we do, we are referring to something done relative to another person and in accordance with a certain kind of equality. For instance, the recompense we owe for some service rendered. We call something 'just', therefore, because we wish to indicate that it possesses the uprightness of justice relative to that in which the action called 'just' terminates, without our considering the manner in which this action has been done by the agent.[47]

In the concept expressed by the word 'just', therefore, the mind abstracts from the intentions and ends of the agent. But, says St. Thomas, 'just' has to be distinguished from 'justice'. Although 'just', taken as a quality of an action, can be considered in itself as something on a par with a measure, that is, as fulfilling a law without more ado, the same is not true of 'justice'. As a virtue 'justice' is thus defined:

> A habit through which we give to all, with a constant, persevering will, that which is just, that is, their right.[48]

Justice is present, therefore, only when the internal will is

[47] *Illud enim in opere nostro dicitur esse justum, quod respondet secundum aliquam aequalitatem alteri; puta recompensatio mercedis debitae pro servitio impenso. Sic ergo justum dicitur aliquid, quasi habens rectitudinem justitiae, ad quod terminatur actio justitiae,* ETIAM NON CONSIDERATO QUALITER AB AGENTE FIAT (*S.T.*, II-II, q. 57, art. 1).

[48] *S.T.*, II-II, q. 58, art. 1.

upright; and that which is just, or right, is formally such when it is joined to justice. 'What is just' is 'the object of justice' — *manifestum est quod jus est objectum justitiae.*[49] Modern philosophers have gone no further than the meaning of the word *justum*, without taking into account the meaning of the word *justitia*, the object of which is 'that which is just.' Hence their mistake.

48. We have to conclude that historians of rational Right must consider the authors of the second period as divided into two great classes. All of them are working to establish the concept of this science and to indicate it in such a way that it is not confused with ethics or with other connected sciences. One class, however, errs through *lack of distinctions*; the other through *excess of distinctions* and abstractions. The first class of authors treats the doctrines of Right as intermingled and mixed with the doctrines of morals; one set of teachings is exchanged for the other. The second class cuts off the doctrines of Right from those of morals so crudely that every communication and relationship between these sciences would be destroyed; the knife of this method would bring nothing but death to these sciences. On the one hand we find Right larded by elements which do not belong to it; on the other hand, Right is made to starve. Authors who support the final death and burial of Right are those who, if you wish, date from Thomasius.

IV.

The extension of rational Right

49. Those who err by unduly enlarging Right offend against the UNITY of this science; those who err by unduly restricting it offend against its UNIVERSALITY. But these are the two characteristics which we have assigned to true philosophy.[50]

[49] *S.T.*, II-II, q. 57, art. 1.

[50] *See* the *Prefaces* to vol. 1 and 2 of the *Opuscoli filosofici* (Milan, 1827–1829), and the *Preface* to the *Nuovo Saggio intorno all'origine delle idee*.

50. The first defect was present in classical times, but not the second, which is far more subtle, far more harmful, and present today. It is easy, in fact, to recognise that in recent times natural Right seems to have been stripped of its most noble element. We are now left with a travesty of Right, which has been confined to external actions and consequently materialised. As a result, Right is necessarily restricted to material things, although to be coherent it also extends to animal actions. It cannot, however, reach up to God. And so the rights of the supreme Being are necessarily banished from a brutalised and atheistic science.

51. This consequence of the principle established long ago by Thomasius was set out in cold terms in the last century, which was entirely devoted to consequences. Everything noble and high-minded, even in pagan antiquity, would certainly have baulked at this. Ancient philosophy recognised no other Right than that which came from God himself; to deny the divinity was to deny Right.

52. Let me offer the sole authority of Cicero as an example of the good sense of antiquity in constantly deriving Right from God. I quote him as a reliable witness to Greek philosophy rather than as a philosopher himself. He knew how to discern the teachings of the Greeks, which he gathered together and recorded in such a brilliant fashion. Allow me, therefore, to quote at length a passage in which this ancient Italian sage leads Right back to its divine source. What he says will also serve as a preface to the present work which deals with the science of rational Right under the title *The Philosophy of Right*. Cicero therefore, with his broad, universal view of things, derives Right from human nature, and shows that both have their origin in God himself.

> This provident, wise, many-faceted, sharp, remembering animal, full of reason and counsel, whom we call 'man', was generated at a certain level of excellence by the supreme God.[51] We see animals of all kinds and species, but only one of them shares in reason and thought, qualities lacking in all the others. But I ask you: what is more divine than reason, not only in human beings, but in the whole of

[51] Here we can see how the supreme God, that is, the true God, was acknowledged even by the pagans.

heaven and earth?[52] And reason, when rendered complete and perfect, is rightly called 'wisdom'. There is nothing better than reason either in human beings or in God;[53] humankind's first society with God is that of reason. But it is necessary that those who have reason in common should also have right reason in common, which is the law. We must, therefore, recognise that human beings and God are associated in the law.[54] And those who share together in *law*, also share together in *right*[55], just as those who have these things in common must be considered as belonging to the same city. If human beings obey the same governments and the same powers, they should much more obey this heavenly order and divine mind and almighty God which is reason.[56] Today, more than ever, this entire world of ours should consider that there is one city common to the gods and human beings. What happens in any city, where the orders of various levels of society are distinguished according to male descent, also takes place in this city in so far as people actually consider themselves as possessing descent and birth from the gods.[57] When we study the entire nature of things, we must come to realise (and this is indeed the case) that after endless movements and revolutions in the heavens a certain stage of maturity was reached for planting the human race whose seed, scattered and sown across the world, was increased by the divine gift of an intelligent spirit. Other things, too, formed part of human life, but were considered as the mortal, frail and weak things that they actually were. The spirit, however, was generated within us by God, and has provided us

[52] Note that the whole of antiquity recognised a divine element in human intelligence.

[53] Every portion of intelligence in human beings is found supremely in God. Cicero himself observes that while God is reason itself, human beings only *share* in reason.

[54] The eternal law is not different from the divine nature: it is *necessity* in God and *obligation* in human beings.

[55] This has to be well understood: human beings cannot fully correspond to God's rights, that is, they cannot give God that which he merits. *See* St. Thomas, *S.T.*, II-II, q. 57, art. 1, ad 3.

[56] I have explained, in *Storia de' sistemi morali*, how this phrase can be rightly interpreted.

[57] Ernest thinks that here the text is corrupt. But I think I have merely rendered it with the meaning proper to the text.

> with descent, genus and kinship (as we can rightly call it) with the heavenly beings.
> Amidst so many kinds of animals, therefore, none possesses any knowledge of God except ourselves. And amongst human beings there is no race so untamed and wild that it does not realise that there must be a God, even if they do not know which God should be theirs. This shows that human beings, who alone know God, remember and as it were understand their genesis. Recall, too, that virtue which is the same for human beings and God, is not found in any other generation of things. Virtue is simply nature as perfect in itself and at its highest point. There is therefore a likeness between human beings and God.[58]

Such is the ample, broad way in which the greatest minds conceived Right. For them, it was indicated and founded in the nature of human beings — this nature possessed reason, which they understood as the trace of God and hence as the primary source, as well as the first subject, of all Rights.

53. If, therefore, we want to profit by the praiseworthy proposal of recent philosophers who have worked hard, precisely and wisely to separate the science of Right from all other sciences, we have at the same time to grasp with the ancient sages the greatness and solidity of what we see spontaneously, and the fullness of thought which always adheres to the substance of things. It is true that the ancients did not pay as much attention and energy to carrying out particular reflections as modern philosophers do, but they never lost their grip on what was essential to every reflection. I think we can respect both aspects of thought by holding carefully to the concept of Right which has already been given. Right consists, as I said, 'in a eudaimonological faculty protected by the moral law.'

Such a faculty is first found in the supreme Being. Human beings and the God from whom they receive their being share the same thing. Our book, therefore, has to deal with rights in their divine source, although briefly, as well as in their human derivation. Such a view of things embraces all rights while distinguishing carefully between ethics, which is concerned with *duties*, and natural Right, which deals with *rights*. The

58 *Laws*, 1, c. 7: 10.

matter of ethics is essentially moral; the matter of natural Right is eudaimonological, as we said, but informed by its relationship with the moral law.[59]

V.

The division of natural Right

54. In this way, the concept of Right as *science* seems to be determined exactly because the concept of right as a *faculty* has

[59] I am glad to have the opportunity here of showing how much I appreciate the sound judgment of Prof. Baroli who was perhaps the first in Italy, after Egger in Germany, to propose the true distinction between *natural Right* and *ethics*. He wrote: 'Of its nature, Right is properly speaking concerned with rights alone (as Egger notes in §6 of his *Private Natural Right*) to which, for the sake of clarification, are added as corollaries, or as an appendix, jural rights. Ethics, therefore, is concerned only with the exposition of duties, of all duties, however, and consequently with jural duties' (*Diritto naturale privato*, §5). I would only add that it is not true to say that 'jural rights' have to appear in natural Right merely as corollaries or as an appendix. This, I think, is not sufficient. For me, *right* exists only in virtue of *duty* which imposes on other human beings respect for the eudemonological faculty that constitutes the matter of Right. We agree, therefore, that natural Right deals with rights alone. But in speaking of rights, natural Right must necessarily deal with *duties* in other human beings. As we said, 'a faculty becomes right in virtue of this relationship with such duties.' Nevertheless, rational Right does not deal with these jural rights in the same way as ethics, which considers them as elements of human morality and deals with them in their entire extension. Rational Right on the contrary considers jural rights merely in the relationship they have with rights, that is, in the relationship which is the *form* of jural rights. — A similar observation can, I think, be made about the way in which Rotteck (*Lehrbuch des Vernunftsrechts* 1. 1. B, §13) distinguishes Right from ethics. According to him that Right is a merely *speculative* science; ethics, on the contrary, is *practical* (the usual abuse of this word). *Right* does not impose obligation; ethics does. I would answer that something can be *moral* (or, as they say, practical) without its being obligatory. There are three forms of moral actions: that which is *licit*, that which is *obligatory*, and that which is *supererogatory*. A licit action is characterised by innocence, that is, it is permitted by the law. Right is not simply licit, as we shall see; it is also *protected* by the moral law. It has an essential relationship to the law and is thus characterised as moral.

[54]

been determined exactly. The treatise must in fact begin from the concept of right as a faculty because only knowledge of this concept enables us to know what Right is as science. As we have said, Right as science is nothing more than 'the doctrine, reduced to its principles, of right as a faculty'.

From this source also, that is, from the correct concept of right as a faculty, springs the division of the science of Right. But in order to go forward clearly, we must first penetrate more deeply the understanding of the concept of the *faculty* we call *right*.

55. By 'faculty' we must not understand simply a physical aptitude for action, but a *permission* or *authority* proceeding from the jural law. In order to avoid confusion on this point, I thought it best to substitute throughout the book the word 'governance' for 'faculty', which is normally used in the definition of right. 'Governance' seems to express better the authority coming from the law. I must repeat that right does not consist in physical action, but in action carried out under the safeguard of the law which forbids others to interfere with that action.

Substituting 'governance' for 'faculty' helps to avoid another possible misunderstanding which could easily be caused by the normal expression. The word 'faculty' seems to signify a mere *potency* of action rather than an *action* itself. But right, as we know, is also inherent to actions. The word 'governance' seems to me suitable for expressing even this facet of right because 'governance' includes the concept of *authority*. It does not entail merely a *potency*, but properly speaking a *quality* also, that is, a quality both of the potencies and of the *acts* of these potencies, and of the *experiences* comprised in these acts.

Right is not something potential, but a quality of actions. This is clearly indicated by the Italian word 'diritto' [and the English word 'right'] which corresponds to the Latin *rectum* from which 'diritto' [and 'right'] was originally transcribed. Just as the 'rightness' of the direction of a line is properly speaking the quality of a line, so 'right' is the quality of an action. I call this quality 'jural' in order to separate it from all other qualities, and by 'jural quality' I mean, therefore, the relationship that the natural or the positive law possesses with that action. This relationship consists in the *protection* accorded to the action against all who might wish to impugn it. Right is a *jural governance, that is, an activity protected by the law* [60] against those who impugn it.

56. It is clear now that if we could classify all activities protected by the moral law, and place them in the most perfect logical order, we would have succeeded in describing from its divine roots and as it were delineating in a wonderful schema the *ideal* proper to jural activity. In this case, we would have put the minor classes of activity below the major classes, and all of them under the most general of all activities; at the same time our understanding would have proceeded logically without omissions or errors of any kind. Our description would have provided the complete, infallible norm of life for the individual, the family, civil society, the State and the human race in a *jurally* perfect manner. All jurally innocent actions would have been traced for these categories of persons. Nothing more would be needed at this point than to *realise* those *ideal* actions held up for universal contemplation.

57. Nevertheless, this ideal of right from which individual and associated persons would be able to deduce their form of life, and live together jurally, would still not embrace the entire doctrine of Right. At the head of that marvellously configured schema of all rights, that is, of all jural activities, would stand the first and most general activity from which all others descend and branch out. It would still be necessary, therefore, to justify this first activity as governance, and to justify every other activity springing from it. In other words, the principal work of philosophy would still have to be carried out: the authority of the law sanctioning this activity would still have to be shown. And if we were to consider this as the work of ethics (which properly speaking reasons about laws)[61] the relationship between *eudaimonological activity* and the law that seals and sanctions it would still have to be demonstrated.

Such a work is outside and anterior to the *ideal* of right; it is the root of the *ideal* of right. It consists in the analysis of the constitutive elements of right and is, I maintain, anterior to the

[60] We always refer to a law which obliges *morally*. Consequently we could also say 'protected by the *moral law*', indicating as *moral* all the laws which induce moral obligation.

[61] Cf. *PE*, *11*.

ideal which can be *realised* in the external actions of individuals, nations and the human race itself.

58. Consequently Hegel's first division of the philosophical science of Right appears to me to be limited and over-restricted by an unnecessary demand for regularity. He posits three parts to this science, the *ideal*, the *conception* and the external *realisation* of right, and requires the second to come from the first, and the third from the second. But that part which is anterior to the ideal of right, that part which is the source of right and the authority of right, or rather which produces the feeling of right, is so proper to the mind and the spirit that it never abandons its primeval throne. It does not manifest itself outwardly through jural and historical actions, but only through symbols, representations and words.

59. I grant that individuals and nations manifest and realise in their interaction the *conception* they have of their own rights, and I grant that their *subjective conception* of mutual rights can be considered as the ideal itself of right (objective right) in so far as this ideal falls within the subject by which it is received and limited. Nevertheless, a distinction has still to be made between the ideal, exemplary right of individual actions, or of several actions bound together, and the *primitive concept* which includes in its simple, universal embrace all possible examples, through which alone it becomes the norm for action. Exemplars themselves have to be distinct and separate (just as actions and their groupings have to be distinct and separate) in order that the latter, like seals and models, may be able to conform to their exemplars. Plato, in his wisdom, was himself aware of this distinction when he posited ειδεα and παραδειγματα.

60. There is a part of Right, therefore, which as higher and more sublime precedes the *ideal* of right and explains it. This reason is never manifested externally, never presented in history. Nevertheless, it is the invisible seed from which the very ideals of all jural actions are produced and draw their own proper substance. This is the part of Right which deals with the *essence* of the concept, that is, the principle common to every right (essence, concept and principle are more or less the same thing here).

61. We also need to note that neither the *ideal* of right nor the

reason behind this ideal differ from the *conception* of right in so far as this conception is just and perfect. The erroneous part of our thoughts about right cannot be called a *conception*, but only a *persuasion* of right. When we speak of a true conception of right, therefore, we can indeed think the reason and the ideal of right first as a mere object, and then as an object intuited by an intelligent subject.

62. This distinction, however, rests on an abstraction, not on a fact. The concept of an object is essentially a contradiction in terms if the object is thought of as never conceived by a mind. The word 'object' itself expresses a relationship with an intelligence, whose term and light it is.[62] It is true that the intelligence to which all ideal objects are referred is essentially the divine, not the human intelligence.[63] Consequently an idea and an ideal can exist without their being communicated to limited, human minds. If, however, the idea and the ideal are communicated to human minds, they cannot undergo any modification whatsoever because reasons and ideas are all immutable. The conception of right is either the reason itself of right, that is, the idea itself of right, or it is not in fact the conception of right.[64] The contingent act of the human mind, although added to the idea, does not alter the knowledge of right in any way; it is something extraneous added to this knowledge.

63. Nevertheless, the *conception* of right differs from the *reason* and the *ideal* of right in so far as the conception is limited in a way unknown to the reason and the ideal. The latter are *per se* unlimited and perfect, but communicated to the human mind in a limited way relative both to their extension and to the intensity of light with which they manifest themselves. If we consider the *conception of right* as a share or *communication in the reason* and *the ideal* of right, we can no longer regard this reason and ideal as having a place in the division of the knowledge of right. Looked at in this way, they remain totally outside the knowledge to which only the *conception* can belong. In other words,

[62] I have touched upon the synthesism intrinsic to the nature of things in several places. Amongst them cf. *PE*, fn. 19.

[63] Cf. *CE*, 1060.

[64] Cf. *Rinnovamento della Filosofia, ecc.*, bk. 3, c. 39–47, for what I have written on the *immutability of ideas*.

the reason and the ideal of right are part of the knowledge of right only in so far as they are contained in this conception.

64. We can, however, think that besides the things which the human mind actually conceives about right, there may be something which it cannot reach because of its limitation. This would allow us to posit a certain negative knowledge or cognition about the reason of right and its ideal.

65. I can now summarise the thoughts which the human mind can have about rational Right. I have examined these thoughts, which include *erroneous persuasions*, and find that they can be reduced to the following major and minor classes:

I. Negative cognition of right which includes:

A. the possibility or the existence of a *supreme reason* of right which, in part, *does not fall* within the human mind;

B. the possibility or the existence of an *ideal* of right which, in part, *does not fall* within the human mind.

II. Positive cognition of right which includes:

A. the *conception*[65] (act of *conceiving*) *of right*, that is, of the way and limit in which

1. there is communicated to the human mind

a) the *supreme reason* of right,

b) the *ideal of right* deduced from the supreme reason;

2. the mind mixes these conceptions with errors (*erroneous persuasions*).

B. the *supreme reason* and *ideal of right* in so far as it is conceived by the human mind, and mixed with errors:

1. the *supreme reason* in so far as it is conceived by the human mind either without errors or mixed with errors;

2. the *ideal* in so far as it is conceived by the human mind either without errors or mixed with errors.

66. And here we have to pause to compare the 'history of philosophical Right' with the 'doctrine of Right itself'. This will enable us to perfect and clarify the division already indicated in the doctrine of Right.

Our science of Right can have for its matter only right as

[65] The word 'conception' has two meanings in common usage. It indicates both the act with which something is conceived, and the thing conceived. Normally, it indicates the thing conceived; but in its proper meaning it expresses the act with which concepts are formed. I use it in this sense here.

conceived and thought by us. If only one thinking mind existed, the schema I have outlined above would contain all that could be written about the rational Right under consideration. But there are in fact many minds which think about right. Every generation has thought about it, and every human being thinks about it now. Some have considered it reflectively, in an ordered fashion, and scientifically. As a result, we have different kinds of *conceptions* and *persuasions* about right. Naturally enough, this provides ample opportunity and material for writing innumerable books in which opinions and systems are brought together. In other words, there is ample scope for writing histories of thought about right. Let me offer a few hints about the division of this kind of history.

67. First, it can be *general* or *limited*. It is general if it deals with all that remains of human thought about right; it is limited if it deals only with certain parts of this thought. In the case of limited histories, the matter may concern either common opinions about right, or simply scientific systems. If common opinions are dealt with, the history may extend to all nations, to several nations, or to one alone; to the whole of time or to certain periods. Scientific history may take as its subject all systems, or those which have appeared in certain parts of the world or at certain periods of time, or even a single system. It is obvious that 'histories of human thought about right' can vary indefinitely in their range. But they can also differ relative to the way in which they are carried. This also has to be considered.

68. It is clear that each intelligence judges the opinions about right espoused by other intelligences according to the norm or rule of right conceived and thought by the one who judges. He or she has no other criterion with which to judge the matter. Consequently, each intelligence — which may be that of an individual, or a society of individuals such as a school of thought, a court of justice, a legislative assembly — takes as the rule and ideal of right whatever right they use and approve. Each philosopher, legislator or historical critic of Right can therefore divide the doctrine of right into two, as far as he is concerned. On the one hand, he possesses the *ideal* and the *conception* of right (the mentally conceived part of right). He raises his own system to the dignity of *ideal*, and considers the opinions of

others as *conceptions* which approximate, more or less, to his system. Nevertheless, it remains certain that here we are dealing with only a relative and subjective ideal, not with one which is absolute and objective. The absolute, objective ideal is unique; relative ideals are as many as there are intelligences to embrace some doctrines of right and discard doctrines proposed by others. This reflection allows us to classify the histories of thought about right according to the way in which the matter has been treated.

69. The history of any doctrine can, therefore, be written in two ways: opinions and systems can simply be expounded, or one doctrine, already embraced by the writer, can be used as the rule and ideal for judging the opinions and systems of others. Recalling the distinction we have already made between a simple jural opinion and a system, and considering that the causes prompting the change and succession of opinions and systems depend upon certain laws and conditions to which humanity is subject, we have the following division of the history of the doctrine of right:

I. *Straightforward histories* (to which the historian adds no judgment of his own), or narratives of

A. jural opinions,

B. jural systems, that is, the science of Right.

II. *Critical histories*, in which the historian is also a philosopher who judges

A. jural opinions,

B. jural systems, that is, the science of Right.

III. *Humanitarian histories* in which historians investigate the laws or the causes by which and according to which change takes place in

A. opinions, and

B. jural systems.

70. It is true, of course, that one system of right can come closer than another to the true, perfect system. But in this case a distinction has to be made between the greater or lesser proximity to perfection and the external reasons which cause us to presume some kind of proximity. Progress can be made both in proximity to perfection and in the external proofs and presumptions in its favour. The nearness of a system to the perfect science of Right can be known only by the individual minds

which perceive its intrinsic reasons; but the progress of ever greater external presumptions, which renders the system more acceptable, depends upon the level of authority which approves this progress.

71. The level of the authority depends upon the number of those who support it and their own individual grade of authority. But each individual's authority itself depends upon intrinsic reasons, or on the weight of some other authority which has to be decided and calculated in the same way. The system itself is capable of becoming more authoritative as it is shown to be older, more diffused and more commonly held. Finally, there is no doubt that the authority of the human race as a whole, which unites in itself everything present in human understanding, is the highest human authority. That author who, a few years ago, considered that the criterion of certainty was to be found in the authority of the human race actually restricted his views to external presumptions in favour of a system without noticing the intrinsic progress — knowable only to individual minds — towards the perfection of the system. Nevertheless, this intrinsic progress gradually harmonises with that of the highest human authority in such a way that the separate judgments of *individual minds* and *public opinion* gradually draw closer across the centuries until they touch. Thus, as time passes, critical histories of human thought about right inevitably acquire a firmer base because the *relative ideal* that philosopher-historians take as the norm of their judgments will always improve in perfection and authority.

72. I must now ask the reader to reflect upon the ample field presented to writers by the history of *jural opinions*, and to fix his attention simply on the great mass of evidence from which those opinions can be gathered, or even upon one single kind of witness, that is, human actions. From this point of view, all human history testifies to the opinions of these generations. In a word, *history*, as Hegel observes, is the *realisation* of right, of the *conception of right*.

73. But history is not the realisation of right alone. Human actions are directed simultaneously by many rules offered to human beings by their intelligence. Only one of these rules is the

jural rule, the principle of right. The historian who investigates human facts under this jural respect, that is, investigates how right, which consists in mental *conceptions* and *persuasions*, is carried out in act, pursues his studies from a single point of view. This aspect differs, for example, from that of the person who studies history relative to ethical or eudaimonological or religious opinions which, by dominating human intelligence at various periods and amongst various nations, regulate human activity.

Whoever decides to undertake a description of human opinions about right must keep in mind that the realisation of right is not of itself history, nor the only characteristic impressed upon human actions. Indeed, that realisation is seen only in certain attitudes of human actions portrayed by history. The historian who loses sight of this will come to believe that history is restricted to his view-point, and that he alone is its vindicator and safeguard.

74. We can now see how close to one another are the *history of right* and the *doctrine of right*. They have many elements in common: opinions and jural systems described by history contain a great deal of truth, all of which necessarily forms part of the doctrine of right if this doctrine is perfect; finding these fragments of truth scattered amongst the history of opinions and systems produces, as we said, a favourable persuasion about the doctrine of right together with a guarantee against error and a weight of authority that must bring the doctrine to the attention of all.

75. We can now continue with our description of the division of the doctrine of philosophical right. So far, we have distinguished two parts in this doctrine, the first centred on the *supreme* jural *reason*, the second on the *relative ideal* of right. The *ideal* consists simply in the derivation of rights from the *supreme reason*. This derivation serves as a type for human actions in so far as they are clothed with some jural quality. The derivation of rights from their principle is, for the author who makes the derivation, the *ideal*. It is *relative* because he cannot see anything better.

76. We now have to add another two parts to our division. They originate as follows. There is only one *principle of right*, but the *special rights* derived from this principle vary because the exterior titles on which they are founded also vary. In Right, as in ethics, it is necessary to distinguish the *law* from the *titles*

which bring it into act.[66] The law is entirely idea; the titles are facts. The law is idea, and nothing more; the titles are facts which, as they change, necessarily require a change in the application and actuation of the law. Consequently, derived right changes also. But these facts, which become *titles* of right by means of the jural law applied to them, are of two kinds: *specific facts* and *individual facts*.

These two classes of facts must be carefully distinguished: specific facts are *ideal*, and constitute the titles of ideal and possible rights which pertain to the theory of right; individual facts are *real* and constitute the titles of *real rights*, which pertain to the extreme realisation of right. For example, the marriage contract is the title of right to conjugal fidelity. But this title can be conceived as *specific* or as *individual*. If the marriage contract is conceived simply as possible, it is specific; in this case it is not simply a fact, but in truth a *species* of fact. Here there is no question of indicating Jane and Mary, or any real people whatsoever, in the marriage contract. Only if the contract is conceived as *individual*, is it considered as realised between two subsisting persons.

77. But two kinds of jural questions, one about rights in theory, the other about rights in act, spring from the distinction between *specific* and ideal *facts*, and *individual* and real *facts*. Questions about theoretical rights consider the existence of *possible rights*; questions about rights in act decide effective cases and judge *real rights*. The first kind of questions asks what the specific rights are; the second asks whether John, a real person, possesses the right which he claims to have. Everything that can be written about derived rights, therefore, can be divided into two vast areas, one embracing *theory*, that is, the specific titles of rights, the other the *realisation* of rights, that is, the individual, real titles of rights. Philosophers and legislators write about the first of these two classes; judges, lawyers, barristers and diplomats about the second.

Jural writings of the second class are not concerned with theory, but are decisions resulting from the application of theory (which is founded on specific titles) to real titles. Jural

[66] Cf. *Storia comparativa de' Sistemi morali*, c. 7, art. 7.

science can, therefore, be divided, as we have in fact divided it,[67] into *pure Right* and *applied* or actuated *Right*. There is no universal, lasting interest in writings about actuated, realised right unless the cases decided refer to the human race as a whole and to succeeding generations. The writings of lawyers and the decisions of tribunals in private affairs do not normally merit much attention; but the books and writings relative to the interests of rulers and nations form part of great libraries and should have a place in any encyclopedia of Right. Nevertheless, the two classes of writings are enclosed in the same sphere, as we have said.[68]

78. We should notice, however, that considerable ability is required in applying *pure Right* correctly to real cases; such an application is the proper work of the expert in jurisprudence. This ability, the art of jurisprudence, although fully attained only with practice, possesses like all other arts certain general rules which together make up a *Theory of the art of the application of Right*.[69] This holds a middle place between *pure Right* and *applied Right* and is used to derive the latter from the former. We now have four parts of the doctrine of right: the principle of Right, derived Right, the art of applying pure Right to real facts, and applied Right. The first three parts are included in the *philosophy* of Right; the first two parts constitute the science of *rational Right*.

79. We still have to say something about the division of rational Right, the principal argument of this present book. We have to describe the more special parts of rational Right, and discover how the principle of Right and the derivation of special rights, of which we have already spoken, are subdivided.

The first of these two parts, which deals with the principle or supreme reason of Right, takes its subdivisions from the elements constituting the *essence of right*. These elements will be enumerated in the treatise itself.

[67] Cf. *SP*, bk. 1, c. 3.

[68] The real rights of governments or States belong to history in so far as they are subsistent facts. Such history could be entitled 'History of real right'. But as arguments in a controversy, they belong to 'applied Right' in the same way as collections of famous trials, etc.

[69] We made the same comment about moral laws in the introduction to *CS*.

The second part, the derivation of special rights, would seem to require as its initial step an examination of the way in which rights are logically derived from the principle, and then an examination of derived rights. But although the separation of these two parts, abstractly considered, seems decisive, its length presents difficulties. The writer cannot deal satisfactorily with the way in which rights are derived from their principle without deriving all of them from that principle. On the other hand, rights which have already been derived cannot be expounded without indicating how they were derived. These two parts cannot be separated, as far as I can see, and I intend to deal with them together.

80. However, one extremely important division must be posited. I have already distinguished *ideal* from *real facts*. When considered in relationship with the jural law, the former constitute the *ideal titles* of rights, and give rise to the theory of rights; the latter constitute *real titles*, and give rise to the *subsistence* of rights.[70] I said that real facts and therefore real titles are varied and contingent, that they may and may not be, that they may be any one of a number of things. The principle of right, however, is one, and always the same. But I did not say whether *ideal facts* which constitute *ideal titles* are subject or not to variation. This investigation is important and necessary if we are to complete the subdivision of derived Right.

It is in fact useless trying to get to the bottom of the matter without thoroughly understanding the logical doctrine which acknowledges the presence of several *modes* in the same *species* of things;[71] these modes are not to be confused with individuals of the species. The species contains in each of its modes all possible individuals, that is, an indefinite number of individuals. With this distinction clearly in mind, it will be easy to understand how a *specific fact*, which puts in being a *specific right* whose title it forms, is able to receive various modes in different periods and states of the human race — modes which then modify the specific title based on the specific fact.

[70] I use the word *subsistence* constantly to indicate the factual *reality* of right. The word *existence* is used to indicate both the real existence (subsistence) and the ideal existence (possibility).

[71] Cf. *The Origin of Thought*, 646-659.

81. Let us take as an example the title we have already used, that is, the marriage contract. From the point of view of the ideal, the marriage contract is not a single fact; it is a species of fact, or as we called it a specific fact. But this marriage contract, although always remaining specifically the same, can receive, and has received various *modes* at different periods in the life of the human race. I am not speaking now of unlawful, but lawful modes. The mode imposed on the marriage contract by the law of perfection, by the Gospel, is monogamy. But the Hebrew legislator had permitted this contract to receive the mode of polygamy. Can the reception of this mode be justified or excused according to natural Right?

82. My answer is this. Perfect love is monogamous. If human nature were perfect, it would be impossible for the marriage contract to receive any other lawful mode than this. The Gospel, therefore, which raises the human race from the depth to which it has sunk and bears it to the heaven for which it is created, had of necessity to lead marriage also to its perfection. But before the Gospel, human beings were imperfect, and capable of imperfect love in so far as they were seduced by the delightful illusions of the senses. As one acute commentator put it recently: 'Love is in inverse relationship to lust.' But the intrinsic substance of the title on which the rights arising from the marriage contract are founded is simply natural love when this substance is considered as a right of nature. Natural love, however, esteems the uniqueness of its object to a greater or lesser degree. If this love, considered as pertaining to nature in general, that is, as relative to the actual state of a given people, is not such that it demands uniqueness and exclusiveness in its object, polygamy will undoubtedly be permitted as long as such a state lasts amongst the people. It will be allowed, even under an inspired legislator, as long as he lacks the power to remove the natural defect inherent in the people — the author of the Gospel had this power, but it was not possessed by anyone before him. Polygamy will be permitted, I maintain, *ad duritiam cordis*, that is, through lack of love in the human heart. And the heart is said to be 'hard' because it cannot love sufficiently to conquer all the caprices of lust.

83. As far as I can see, this example shows clearly that specific rights change according to the periods in which the human

race exists. It is not sufficient, therefore, to establish a single mode of these rights, which have to be considered in the entire course of a nation's history — a difficult, immense work indeed[72] which is certainly too much for my own weak forces and would require an entire association of learned jurists, an entire historico-philosophical school. But perhaps I could remind Italy of her ancient calling?

84. Nevertheless, I cannot entirely omit — in a work which I have dared to call *The Philosophy of Right* (although the benevolent reader will kindly take this as an indication of the tendency of the book rather than a strict promise on my part) — the part which deals with the changeableness of specific rights springing from the changeableness of the titles on which they are founded.

85. The need for clarity, therefore, prevents my dealing with all the modes of a specific right when I deal with the specific right itself. But it will help if we divide 'derived Right' into two parts, one of which will deal with the derivation and description of the *species* of these rights. These species will be indicated according to one of their modes, and if possible according to the best of these modes. In other words, I shall deal with the right as it is expressed in modern times and in our nation. The other part will show the variety of modes in which that species of right can be presented in any part of the human race.

86. For the moment, however, I have to exclude the second part. Its importance and dignity prevent my dealing with it as adequately as it deserves. I shall, however, consider the first part very carefully. Its various branches can then serve once more as a schema and index of the second part.

[72] As we have already seen, 'the history of opinions and jural systems' has something in common with the 'doctrine of Right'. In the same way, 'the humanitarian history of Right', as we call it, has something in common with this part of 'the doctrine of rights' which deals with the *various modes* according to which specific rights can come into being. However, the doctrine depends upon the history only to the extent that the history is used to stimulate the philosophical imagination in its quest for possible cases (although this imagination is not limited to historical cases). History, on the other hand, describes only the facts in which the modes of right are encountered, or at most the causes of these facts in the different conditions of the human race.

87. In the treatise on the derivation and classification of rights we first discuss the distinction between *connatural* and *acquired* rights. The two most general modes of acquisition depend upon the act of a single person and the acts of two or more persons. Both kinds of acts can either bring into being entirely new rights or modify already existing rights. Moreover, two or more persons can act in concert without the establishment of a true contract in such a way that their simultaneous acts can result in titles of right. These persons could also make true contracts which in affecting only the objects of right have the effect of modifying existing rights, but in affecting the subjects themselves of rights bring new rights into existence. Such contracts are social contracts and the source of *social Right*, a vast branch of the doctrine of derived rights.

This sketch enables us to see that social Right, despite its immense breadth and importance, is not scientifically speaking one of the first two parts of the doctrine of Right (although it is often considered as such). The whole of Right is divided into *private* and *public* right, and social Right is rather a branch of right growing from the other branches which precede it.

88. I shall speak later about what we call 'private Right' as distinct from 'public Right' because this terminology is not altogether correct. For the moment it is sufficient for me to insist on something that springs from long consideration: if we are going to disentangle the intricacies of human rights, it is indispensable to abandon useless abstractions and fictitious entities, which result from the way we conceive things mentally, in order to establish the principle that 'the subject of every right is always the individual'. We have to reduce to individual rights even those rights which we call, for the sake of abbreviation, 'social rights'. There are not two subjects, the individual and the social body, which are capable of right, but a single subject, the human individual. However, this does not prevent our using the names *individual Right* and *social Right* if we find this convenient. The importance of this clarification of ideas will be seen at length in its appropriate place.

89. If we now add the division of 'social Right', and make a synopsis of what has been said above about the more general divisions of the doctrine of Right, we have the schema shown overleaf.

SCHEMA OF THE PHILOSOPHY OF RIGHT

THE PHILOSOPHY OF RIGHT

FIRST PART
The principle, that is,
essence of right
(Positive and negative knowledge, as on page 45)

SECOND PART
DERIVED RIGHT
(*Method of deriving rights. — Derived rights*).

THIRD PART
Science of the art of applying right to real titles (4)

Division 1.

SPECIFIC RIGHTS.

NATURAL RIGHT — INDIVIDUAL RIGHT

1. CONNATURAL RIGHTS (in God, in human beings). — Connatural freedom. — Connatural ownership.
2. ACQUIRED RIGHTS. — Acquired freedom. — Acquired ownership
 Sect. 1. Through the ACT OF A SINGLE BEING (whether this act pertains to an individual or a society (1))
  A. in God (title of *creation*);
  B. in human beings who with their acts produce
   1) NEW RIGHTS (titles of *occupancy* and of *generation*), or
   2) MODIFICATIONS of preceding rights.
 Sect. 2. Through CONNECTED ACTS OF MORE THAN ONE BEING (whether these acts pertain to individuals or to moral bodies)
  A. *WITHOUT ANY CONTRACT*, or

AGREED RIGHT — SOCIAL RIGHT

  B. *THROUGH A CONTRACT* regarding only
   1) the OBJECTS of right (in which case it simply modifies existing rights), or
   2) the SUBJECTS themselves of right through association which produces state of society: while this state lasts, we have
    I. SOCIAL RIGHT, which is
     A. GENERAL (common to all societies)
      1) INTERNAL, right of the members of the social body relative to one another. — Civil right;
      2) EXTERNAL, right of the members of the society relative to its government, and vice-versa; (2)
     B. SPECIAL (proper to individual kinds of society).
      1. Right of societies which have as their aim the attainment of CERTAIN RIGHTS. — Conjugal society. — Parental society. — Societies for work, — business societies, etc.
      2. Rights of societies, which have as their aim the regulation of the MODALITIES of rights, their defence, — their better co-existence, etc.
       a) *partial.* — Assurance societies etc.
       b) *universal.* — CIVIL SOCIETY.
    II. EXTRASOCIETAL SOCIETY, that is, Right independent of association, conserved in individual associates during their association (3).

Division 2.

MODES OF SPECIFIC RIGHTS,
that is, MODIFICATIONS WHICH RIGHTS UNDERGO
WITHOUT LOSING THEIR SPECIFIC IDENTITY
AS A RESULT OF HUMANITARIAN DIFFERENCES
(*same subdivision as that of division 1*)

Notes for the Schema of the Philosophy of Right

(1) This final part is attributed in the usual divisions to *public, external Right*. But the rights are the same whether their subject is an individual or a moral body. If rights are not founded in a contract stipulated between moral bodies, these bodies, relative to one another, are as individuals in the state of nature. Cf. *SP*, bk. 1, c. 10

(2) Government is external to society, as I have shown in *SP*, *loc. cit*. This division must then be repeated in the Right of every special society.

(3) Cf. *SP*, bk. 1, c. 11

(4) I cannot display in this work the entire canvas of the *Philosophy of Right* and consequently cannot describe in detail the complete division of what I actually present. I shall content myself with what follows, offering first an introduction and exposition of the moral system, and dividing the whole work into four principal parts which will deal with:

1. the *essence* of right;
2. the *principle of derivation* of rights;
3. *derived Right*, and
4. the different *modes* which derived Right takes as a consequence of humanitarian varieties.

I shall then subdivide derived Right in two, that is, into *individual Right* and *social Right*.

VI.

Aids to the study of the philosophy of Right

90. The *Schema of the Philosophy of Right* should itself be sufficient to demonstrate the breadth of this study. Realising that this investigation is a part of philosophy already shows us that the correct use of reason is the only means with which the subject can be grasped. But human reason needs assistance to awaken, direct and strengthen it, and to provide it with matter for its exercise.

91. Jural philosophers receive the matter of their considerations from the observation of facts, and from the accurate examination of the relationships in which human beings are found and have been found. These relationships enable philosophers to imagine other relationships of the same kind. Such facts and relationships are brought to the attention of the mind principally by prolonged acquaintance with human affairs and solid knowledge of historical relationships. In other words, principally by the 'history of humanity'.

92. But when reason is presented with these facts and relationships — jural cases which it is called upon to decide, as it were — it has scarcely taken the first step. It still needs help to make *good* decisions. The assistance it receives at this point may be *practical* or *theoretical*. Practical assistance can be reduced to the habit and acquired feeling for deciding cases which comes when a person has had experience in settling disputes and quarrels. Theoretical assistance springs principally from the following sciences:

I. *Anthropology*, both *natural* and *supernatural*, which reveals completely to the jural philosopher the natural and supernatural states of human nature in all its variety.

II. *Positive right at various periods and in various nations*. This positive right may be written, or based on use. The *philosophy of positive Right*, that is, the study of the motives which have led different legislators to make law, is especially useful here in helping the mind to discover more surely the decisions required in different cases.

III. The *histories of rational Right* which we have classified above.[73] These also are of great assistance to the mind in this work.

IV. *Politics*, and the *philosophy of politics*.

V. *Theoretical philosophy*, especially logic and critique. Finally

VI. *Ethics*, which has a special relationship with Right. This last science must be to the forefront in the mind of anyone wishing to make progress in jural philosophy. As we have said, right is 'governance protected by the moral law'.

Before everything else, therefore, we must know the theory of the moral law: we have to be familiar with duty, from which right is derived, and with the nature and force of moral obligation.

I have already dealt with these matters at length in appropriate works,[74] but feel I can help my readers by offering some considerations on moral philosophy as an introduction to this treatise on rational Right. Readers who are already familiar with the subject can omit this. But the brief section is given here for those who would like to use it.

[73] Cf. *65*.

[74] Under the heading *Filosofia della Morale*.

MORAL SYSTEM

93. This brief exposition will be divided into three sections: 1. an exposition of the system which I have made my own; 2. an exposition of the most noted systems, with a comparison between them and the system already explained; 3. some considerations on the natural relationships between morals and religion, and on the way in which religion brings morals to its fulfilment.

SECTION ONE

THE PRINCIPLE AND ESSENCE OF MORALITY

I.

The faculty of knowledge is partly necessitated and partly free

94. The moral system that I have proposed requires first of all the existence in the human being of a faculty of judgment which can be exercised freely.[75]

Interior observation shows that such a faculty does indeed exist. Not all our acts of judgment are necessary, nor are they all determined by the irresistible light of truth. We often judge interiorly in a way contrary to the truth we do indeed see. The force of our free decision moves us in this direction by applying unjust, domineering pressure in favour of this judgment and contrary to the truth.

Thus we fall into error, a phenomenon otherwise inexplicable in a reasonable nature. Our error is the evil fruit of our will, not of our intellect.

95. Nevertheless, our *free* judgments do not impede the presence of other, *necessary* judgments. Not all human judgments are chosen by free decision; many are formed by our intelligent nature before free decision can operate. As intelligent beings, we *apprehend* things before our will can influence and act on our *persuasion* precisely because it is necessary for us to

[75] Cf. *PE*.

know before we can go on to want or reject what we have come to know. When we apprehend things, which are then loved or not loved, desired or abhorred by the will which judges them good or unsavoury, we perform an intellectual operation that precedes all voluntary and free judgments. There are, therefore, two ways of knowing in human beings: *free knowledge* and *necessary knowledge*.

96. Necessary knowledge precedes free knowledge; free knowledge is always produced by a judgment made about that which is necessarily known beforehand.

97. In forming a judgment, we can make decisions by considering under various aspects the things we know. For the moment, let us confine our attention to those judgments we make about the worth or degrees of goodness of what we know.

We can judge that something known by us has a certain value or determined goodness only if, in contemplating the concept we have formed of that object, we find in it that worth or goodness which we attribute to it. But the concept or apprehension of this object appertains to our necessary way of knowing things, not to our free knowledge. As we said, our first apprehension of objects is not subject to the power of the will, but acts in us spontaneously, in virtue of the very laws that govern our understanding.

If therefore we cannot but discover in the apprehension of an object the degrees of goodness which we attribute to it, it must be the case that in our apprehension of the object, which is the first operation of our spirit, we already apprehend also all the goodness and all the worth that we then freely attribute to it. But precisely because this second operation of our spirit is free, and not necessary, it is able not only to conform to, but also dissent from, or stand contrary to the first operation, that is, to the apprehension. In this case, we attribute to objects degrees of goodness that are not present in the concepts we have of them, or we deny them the degrees of goodness that are contained in that concept.

This is the origin of truth and falsity in our judgment. Considered relatively to the free will that produces the judgment, this is also the origin of moral good or malice in that judgment. If our faculty of free judgment is upright, it will reaffirm what has been seen by the faculty of necessary apprehension; it will acknowledge the degree of goodness which it has apprehended in the objects, without making any effort to disturb or alter it.

98. If, on the other hand, our faculty of free judgment is distorted — if, for example, it is misled and confused by passion — we begin to lie to ourselves. Although we behold objects faithfully depicted before the mind on the canvas of the soul[76] as they actually are (this is the work of the faculty of apprehension), we do not want to acknowledge them in their legitimate, natural colours. It is as though we had something wrong with our eyes, and saw things mixed up and wrongly coloured. This consideration leads to an important truth: that is, there is always a foundation of truth in us, although sometimes error and perverted judgment prevail. We then see what we do not see, and feel what we do not feel. Our mind is lost in an inextricable labyrinth of sophisms, while our heart reproves our every step, telling us that we bear the manifest truth sculpted as it were within. Our eyes, constrained forever to see truth, can only avoid it if we constantly try to tear them away from it.

99. It must be granted therefore that we are not free to see or not see the truth presented to us by our faculty of apprehension which receives and holds within itself the objects offered to it; at the same time, it must also be granted that we are then free to *acknowledge* these objects, their dignity and their degree of excellence without altering or counterfeiting them. This is the work of the faculty which enables us to judge their worth, and it is this faculty which is subject to the violence of our passions. The eye of this faculty can be distorted, obscured and darkened by the murk diffused by the passions. But the simple faculty of direct, primitive knowledge preserves in us a profound cognition of truth in the midst of a thousand errors because it receives objects in itself as they are and as they act in the spirit. It is the faculty of reflective, subsequent knowledge which makes us meander through the ways of sophistry, error and illusion. inducing us to obstinately deny to ourselves what we actually see, hear and touch.

100. Once and for all, therefore, we have to distinguish *knowledge* from *acknowledgement*. When human beings perceive an

[76] This metaphor is not out of place. We use it as a way of indicating the intellectual adherence of objects to the soul, nothing more.

object, they immediately know it for what it is; this is the act of simple knowledge. But when we turn our gaze to the object we have perceived and say to ourselves, 'Yes, it is such, it does have this value', we *acknowledge* it and reaffirm it to ourselves; we reaffirm by means of an active, willed act what we already know by means of a necessary, passive act. This is our act of reflective cognition.

101. One of the principal distinctions between these two acts can be described as follows. The first, proper act of our faculty of knowledge consists simply in *perceiving*. More generally speaking we always apprehend[77] an object whole and entire. We take nothing from it, and indeed distinguish nothing within it. For us, it is one and simple; we notice it as it is. But when we come to the second act, we have the power to acknowledge the object wholly or in part. We can judge every individual quality of the object, and from a single point of view. In a word, with our first faculty we see the object in a unique, determinate mode; with the second we see it in different modes, either as a whole or in any one of its least elements, its most abstract qualities and its most distant relationships.

102. Moreover, with the first act of necessary knowledge we acquire the concepts of things and contemplate their essences.[78] We cannot err about these essences which as *anticipations* precede all the partial judgments that we form about things. Let us take as an example Carneades' famous argument against the existence of justice.

This famous philosopher, the founder of the third Academy, certainly possessed the idea of justice, and would have been able to point to it in himself, describe it correctly and re-affirm it if he had succeeded in maintaining his reflection undisturbed. But he added an arbitrary quality to justice when he called it *stupid*. This abitrary affirmation, this calumny, destroyed justice. But

[77] Apprehension is more general than *perception*. The latter requires that the object be a *real* being which exercises its action by making us feel some degree of its *power* which becomes the basis of perception itself. *Apprehension* on the other hand is carried out by the understanding apart from this action. It is sufficient that in some way or other we acquire the concept of a being even if this being does not *really* act upon us.

[78] The word *essence* should be taken in the sense attributed to it in *OT* 646, where it has been defined as 'that which is contained in the idea of the thing'.

Carneades was at war with himself. After having affirmed justice, he had to confess that he felt or knew it. If not, he could not even have spoken about it. In effect, he denied knowing justice by means of a judgment which depended upon the way in which he directed his reflections and his will.[79]

II.

Morality begins in that part of our knowledge-faculty which remains free

103. The exercise of human choice begins, therefore, in the faculty by means of which we acknowledge things. Prior to this faculty there exist in us only first, non-deliberate, spontaneous movements which are proper to the faculty of basic knowledge.

104. But the principle of morality must necessarily be sought where we find the principle of choice; it can manifest itself neither before nor after the free activity of human beings, but only along with this activity to which it has an intrinsic, necessary relationship. The principle of morality is simply the supreme norm that must guide human choice and freedom in its various undertakings.

105. Choice and freedom are not manifested, therefore, until

[79] 'When he (Carneades) divided *justice* into two parts, one of which he called civil *justice* and the other natural *justice*, he destroyed both. According to him, civil wisdom exists, but is not *justice*; natural *justice* also exists, but is not wisdom' (Lactantius, bk. 5, c. 16). — Carneades possessed the notion of *justice*, but could deduce it only from utility. This was a fairly common opinion in weak, pagan philosophy because it seemed to be the only way of avoiding the description 'stupid'. False judgments of this kind clearly indicate outrageous contradictions whose effect was to lead discouraged minds into scepticism. Lactantius is quite clear about this (c. 17): 'Carneades realised what the nature of *justice* was and did not have to look far to see that it was not stupidity. I think I know where he made his mistake, however. He did not really think that just persons were stupid; he knew they were not, but did not understand why they were not. He wanted to show that the truth was hidden in order to defend what he asserted in his teaching, the height of which was to maintain that nothing can be perceived.'

the faculty by which we acknowledge things has been activated. In its turn, morality makes its first appearance in the human spirit when the first free act of acknowledgement is posited. Consequently the first voluntary acknowledgement of objects we have apprehended is the first moral act, an act which is completed within the spirit and expressed in the form of right judgment. All other acts relative to morality depend upon this first act, as we shall show. It is true to say, therefore, that every sin we commit, without exception, has as its root a evil thought,[80] and we can conclude that the first form of both morality and immorality is always a judgment, that is, an acknowledgement or disavowal of our preceding cognitions.

We also have to say that we feel ourselves obliged by an eternal and insuperable law to *acknowledge* faithfully what we *know*; we have to judge in accord with the faculty of first knowledge. This law is so founded in the nature of things that we cannot even conceive that the opposite is possible. This law simply tells us that we have to affirm to ourselves that we see what we see, that we perceive what we perceive and nothing else. With our knowledge-faculty we perceive or apprehend an object; with the faculty by which we acknowledge things, we are required, by the nature of this faculty, to say simply: 'Yes, we perceive it.' Our faculty of acknowledgement requires us to testify to ourselves that we cannot do otherwise, although we can freely try to hide from the eye of the soul what we know.

Our first, supreme duty, therefore, is to adhere to the TRUTH, and to witness interiorly to what is true by acknowledging it to ourselves and saying: 'I know this; it is so.'[81]

106. The voice of this law of truth impressed by God in our hearts will continually be better heard if we consider the effects it produces in us, effects which can also be considered as its natural sanction.

[80] Jesus Christ, in describing how sins spring from the inner life of human beings, puts EVIL THOUGHTS as the first of all blameworthy acts (Matt 15: 19).

[81] Holy Scripture offers its greatest praise of the divine law when it defines and expounds its essence with these few words: YOUR LAW IS THE TRUTH (*justitia tua, justitia in aeternum, et lex tua veritas*, Ps 118: 142 [Douai]). In harmony with these words, Scripture says: 'IT IS JUSTIFIED IN ITSELF' (*Judicia Domini vera, justificata in semetipsa. Ibid.*).

The simple, just acknowledgement of what we know is pleasant because human nature does not have to strain to achieve it. The opposite is true when we disavow what we know and alter it for ourselves; here a violent, absurd and rash effort is needed, the effect of which is war and agitation within our spirit. If the things we acknowledge are good, they produce *joy* in us; if they are bad, *sorrow*. But the act itself of acknowledgement is never distasteful; its veracity always provides a source of pleasure.

Pleasure is found again in the good order that the act itself places and produces in what the intellect knows, and in the harmony and union that the act brings about among the affections of the spirit. It is indeed true, as far as the intellect is concerned, that the right judgment we make about the things we know does not strip these things of their prerogatives, nor bestow upon them prerogatives which are not theirs. All the objects, depicted as it were in the faculty with which we apprehend things, are placed in their natural order by our act of acknowledgement, which lodges them in their proper place according to the degrees of entity they share. In other words, they take their place according to their dignity and according to the value they merit. The order in our understanding is thus maintained, confirmed and completed.

107. The same can be said about the unity of our affections. If the two faculties of knowledge and acknowledgement are in harmony, the human being possesses a single love, esteem, contempt and hate. But if these faculties are at odds with one another — and this is the case when the second faculty refuses to accept as good what the first has perceived as good, and tries with all its might to see evil in that good — the absurd contradiction and struggle present in the mind is re-enacted in the human spirit. Two contrary loves and hates battle with one another; the love and hatred found in the depths of our being where, although almost suffocated, it is a necessary effect of the faculty of direct knowledge, and another, opposite love and hatred which although frenetic, superficial and almost on the periphery of the spirit, stifles and impedes the cries of the first as it tries in vain to awaken us to the truth. Plunged into misery, we then love what we should hate, and hate what we should love. Our intellective feeling dictates one thing; the seduced will

and the seducing judgment dictate another. We thus become an enigma to ourselves.

These different feelings of peace and joy, of war and strife, are like reverberant voices with which the law of justice naturally makes itself heard by human beings in all its authority, lovableness and power.

III.

Morality expands from the faculty of free knowledge to the affections of the spirit and to external actions

108. When the moral faculty by means of which we acknowledge things is in accord with the faculty of simple (direct) knowledge, the spirit too, which is not unjust of itself, honours or rather has already begun to honour the truth. In this state, the spirit pays reasonable, well-ordered respect and affection to the objects set out before it according to the degree of entity, that is, of dignity with which they are furnished.

Here we must note that no prior reason explains this action on the part of the spirit except the human being's very nature,[82] which is constituted in such a way that it spontaneously loves things in proportion to their goodness, that is, in proportion to the goodness it has practically, or freely, known in them.

109. Moreover, the question is not simply reduced to that of agreement or natural correspondence between the *practical* judgments about the worth of things, and the *affections* of the spirit. These affections are matched and prolonged both by commands through which human beings operate externally and through animal feelings and instincts arising from feelings. Such instincts themselves produce movements and actions in the matter which forms the human body.

We can only marvel at the wonderful bond between the different parts of the human being, and at the awesome multiplicity

[82] There is undoubtedly a higher reason which shows that this cannot be otherwise. But this is part of *Ontology*.

and unity of this being. Imagine, for instance, that a *freely chosen judgment* produces some opinion in me about the goodness of an object that I have perceived. As quick as lightning, an *affection* proceeds from that judgment. The affection arises in my spirit without any action on the part of my will and, despite its wholly spiritual quality, causes my heart to beat faster, my face to light up with love, my lips to smile, and finally my limbs to tremble. All these parts of the body express the same affection, and they would seem to be competing to help me so that I can either possess a good I love but do not have, or enjoy blissfully some good I already possess.

110. *Dynamic* is the word I have used to describe the connection between the judgment (first effect of the volitive force) and the affections of the spirit, between the affections of the spirit (second effect) and the corporeal feelings, between the corporeal feelings (third effect) and external operations (the fourth effect of the same volitive force). This connection is in fact a real force by means of which the volitive judgment effectively arouses the power of spiritual affections. These in turn move the corporeal feelings which then generate instincts, movements and actions.[83]

111. We have, therefore, a natural connection or movement which is propagated so rapidly from one human power to another — from link to link, as it were — that the formation of the first practical judgment is almost the same as loving or hating, or feeling pleasure or pain, or acting externally in various ways. Given this connection, it is also clear that morality must propagate and extend to the human faculties. Morality is a duty imposed not only on the first faculty of practical judgment, which sees its object, but also on all other faculties by means of which we love and act, despite their blindness. If I am morally obliged to move in a given way the first link in the chain, it is evident that I am equally obliged to furnish all the other links with those movements which arise from the first link. If I am obliged to acknowledge what is good, I am also obliged to love it (I could not acknowledge it without loving it), and to act in a way corresponding to this love (I could not love it if I did not act in this way). The three things are indeed intimately

[83] Cf. *Storia de' Sistemi Morali*, and *AMS*.

connected. It is true that affection of itself is blind and necessary; it is true that our external actions, materially understood, are furnished neither with reason nor with intelligence; nevertheless, the obligation imposed upon the free intelligence alone is sufficient to subdue and order in like manner our affections and actions in so far as they are necessary consequences of freely *chosen* acts of my intelligence. Intelligence as *freely chosen* serves as sight to the other powers whose goodness or moral guilt depends on the goodness or evil of such sight.

112. Thus, everything within human beings becomes moral because the first cognitive activity, on which all the rest physically depends, is itself essentially moral.

IV.

Comments on the power of the will over a part of the faculty of knowledge

113. This theory is based on the first fact we have observed: 'The will has some power over a part of the faculty of knowledge.' And the part of the faculty of knowledge over which the will exercises its hidden, but powerful influence is that with which we judge the worth and goodness of the things that the faculty has apprehended. We call this our *practical* judgment because it is moved by the force of the *will*, that is, by the principle of human action. This judgment must be distinguished from the *theoretical judgment* which is stimulated only by the light of *truth*. *Truth*, which sometimes activates the spontaneity of our judgment, terminates in this theoretical judgment to which its action is confined.

114. We have to understand that if we do not wish to admit practical judgment, a judgment activated by the will, we have consequently to deny all will and all freedom. Will and freedom either have their place in our judgment, or are totally lacking in human nature. This can easily be seen if we consider that our physical activities cannot be free unless carried out as a consequence of the decree of a will which knows and wants them.

But the will cannot want them unless it has previously judged them as good. These activities are not free of themselves, therefore, but are free because the will which judges them to be good is free, and hence wants them.

The same can be said about our affections. Taken by themselves, without any connection with a will which moves them freely, they are blind phenomena; freedom and will are extraneous to them. But as soon as the rational will attaches itself to affections, they become willed and free; the will, having declared them good, approves and stimulates them. Our judgment about the goodness of things precedes and informs the affections and operations we call 'willed'. It is in this judgment that the will first unfolds its power to reign over and command the lower powers.

115. The many errors against freedom originate from the false supposition that all judgments are necessary, and that judgment about things never lies within our free power.

116. If Spinoza, Collins and Jansen had considered the distinction between the two faculties of *apprehension* and of *reflection* on the things we apprehend and judge, they would have easily found a way to escape from the labyrinth of sophistry in which their denial of human freedom had entangled them.[84] In their eyes, there is only one way of knowing things; they were oblivious to another great, highly important fact proper to the human spirit, the fact that we acknowledge things with practical force. And we have to admit that there can be no place for human freedom when only simple, direct knowledge is seen in

[84] The argument which misled Collins in his *Dissertazione contro la libertà umana* [Inquiry concerning Human Freedom] begins from the principle that 'the will is determined by the intellect'. According to Episcopius 'this is the rock against which the ablest defenders of freedom have come to grief, and to which they have no answer.' That apparently awesome objection would have been resolved easily if sufficient distinction had been made between the faculty of *knowledge* and the faculty of *acknowledgement* in the intellect. It could have been shown that one of these two parts of the understanding was subject to necessity, and the other guided by freedom. In fact, experience shows us that our thought contains something which is free and something which is not free. This explains why both the defenders and adversaries of freedom appeal to experience in their own favour. But distinguishing the two intermingled elements enables us to see the exact limits of truth and error in these systems.

the human mind without any reference at all to reflective acknowledgement. In fact, simple, primitive knowledge is not free; it is passive, receiving as it were, without acting. It absorbs truth, that is, the ideas or essences of things, as they present themselves.

This system, which denies freedom because it eliminates freedom's essential power to assent to or dissent from the truth, which is its essential act, renders error inexplicable in human beings. Hobbes himself denied freedom by reducing it to nothing.[85]

117. Others on the contrary grant too large a part to error present in the human spirit. Their observation is deficient in the opposite sense. They do not reflect that our immediate cognitions are provided by nature itself and are therefore infallible

[85] The mistake into which Hobbes was led by his subtle explanations about the nature of error has its origin in his failure to distinguish between the faculties of knowledge and acknowledgement, a failure he had in common with many other philosophers. Hobbes came to the conclusion that truth and falsity cannot exist except in the words with which propositions are expressed. Words, he says, are arbitrarily imposed upon things by us; the first truths simply depend upon the arbitrary decision of those who first used words (*Logic*, c. 3, n. 7–8). This system could not be avoided once it was admitted that the first ideas were known to human beings and that the whole of knowledge originated from the analysis of these ideas. This analysis was accepted as a *necessary* process to which human beings could not deny their assent (c. 6). Once posited, Hobbes' principle allowed no possibility of error to the human mind, in which everything was determined. Error could be found only in a collision in the wrong application of words. If Hobbes had observed the presence in human beings of a *free power* of assent to or dissent from what is true, a power capable of disturbing the attention of the spirit and hence of altering our very cognitions by creating *opinions* and *persuasions*, he would have noticed immediately that falsehood does not lie in words alone. He would have realised that it is found in the affirmations, whether expressed or not in words, of internal judgments not in conformity with things. In fact, he was unable to deny human self-deception (c. 5), but attributed it to his false principle that 'a thing is signified by a sign which does not signify it.' It is extraordinary that after seeing how a person can deceive himself by wrongly interpreting a sign, Hobbes cannot take one further step and advert to the *power of free decision* which is also enclosed within that error. If we can deceive ourselves through the power of free decision, by interpreting badly the signs of things, can we not equally deceive ourselves by uniting or separating badly our ideas and assents?

precisely because our power of free decision is completely absent from the formation of such cognitions.

118. Let us imagine that two people, who have both seen Trajan's column, offer estimates of its height. One of them hates Rome and is inclined to detract from its grandeur; he will tell you that the column is lower than it actually is. The other admires Rome and wants to extol it as much as he can; this is enough for him to elevate the height of the column out of all proportion. Both of them are wrong in their estimate of the height of the column, although both of them actually possess the type of what is true. The image of the column was received equally by both of them through the medium of their sense organs without the intervention of their free decision. The first idea they form of the column as a whole is equal in both. But they begin to disagree when they reflect on the image they have of the column and calculate its approximate height. The one who wants to keep it as low as possible makes his calculation according to his free decision and maintains that it is five metres lower than it actually is; the other, who also wants to make the calculation depend upon his estimation of things, decides that it is five metres higher than it actually is. There is therefore some part of the truth which is necessarily received in the minds of both these persons; and there is also in both of them something false created by their free decision.

119. By establishing that one part of human cognitions is always unfailingly and necessarily true, we have annihilated scepticism; by establishing that another part can be falsified by our free decision, we defend the existence of truth, the possibility of error, and morality.[86]

[86] Leibniz is among the few who have recognised the immense power of the human will to move the judgments of the understanding in one way rather than another. — Amongst more recent authors, G. Burlamachi admitted this power without any hesitation, as we can see in his *Principi di Diritto naturale*, p. 1, c. 1, §12 and c. 2, §4–9, but without taking advantage of it as he could have done. In fact, he was a *subjectivist*, and believed that law and obligation could be deduced from the happiness towards which human beings are ordered, rather than from the authority of what is true itself.

The Scottish school, ignoring the existence of free knowledge, the seat of morality, was obliged to recur to a new *faculty* in order to explain moral obligation. This faculty was devised for the purpose and called 'moral'.

V.

The moral law: its objective necessity and its eternity

120. What has been said shows that the first act of justice is to judge things rightly in so far as this depends upon our will.[87]

Right judgment is formed by our acknowledging things as they are in our apprehension, without any desire on our part to increase or diminish their goodness, excellence and dignity. Our faculty of judgment naturally feels itself obliged to harmonise with our faculty of apprehension because such harmony consists only in acknowledging the truth. It is manifestly contradictory and absurd to judge that something is different from what we know it to be. But in so far as this contradiction and *absurdity* are willed, they are *moral evil* itself; on the other hand, and in so far as it depends upon our will, the absence of such dissent, and the agreement between what we *affirm* and what we *know*, is *moral good*.

121. The *absurdity* of moral evil and the *truth* of moral good can

Dugald Stewart, in his synopsis of moral philosophy (Edinburgh, 1793), dedicates the second part to examining the active and moral faculties of the human spirit. After saying that he believes it absurd to ask why we are obliged to conform our actions to the rules of virtue, he makes use of a *moral conscience* as a supreme rule, or better as a moral necessity. He attributes to Butler the honour of being the first amongst the moderns to base morals upon this fundamental principle. He concludes: 'From what we have said, it appears that the *moral faculty*, considered as an active faculty of the human spirit, differs essentially from all the faculties which we have already listed' (c. 1, sect. 6, art. 3). In the system we have expounded, there is no need for any arbitrary supposition about such a mysterious, hidden faculty which presides over morality in human beings. 'The moral element, according to us, consists in the relationship between the faculty of perception or knowledge with the faculty of practical judgment or acknowledgment of what is true.' Because we are *free* in such judgments, we feel ourselves strictly obliged by the force of truth: and this is 'moral obligation', resulting from 'the relationship of what is true with a being free to acknowledge what is true.' By transgressing or carrying out this duty, human beings become morally evil or morally good. Malice or probity is the effect of the execution or transgression of duty, or 'the relationship between human action and obligation.'

[87] The great commandment repeated so often in the Scriptures: JUDGE RIGHT THINGS, YOU SONS OF MEN (Ps 57: 1 [Douai]).

be seen more clearly if we consider the *immutability* and *eternity of essences*, which can never be changed from what they are.

Considered in relationship to the different acts of our spirit, immutability and eternity furnish us with the concept of the *identity of things*, the final reason for the necessity we experience in the truth of our judgment, and for the disorder that we feel present in the falsity of our judgment. It is through their identity that things are constant to themselves in their metaphysical entity, that is, are what they are.

122. However, this expression, *identity of things*, does not denote any peculiar quality relative to things themselves. As we said, it expresses only a relationship with our way of looking at them, that is, with the multiplicity of the acts in which we continually see them. If our faculty of knowledge and of acknowledgement always had these things present, and contemplated them with a single, uninterrupted act, we would never speak about their identity. But we do in fact look at them intellectually, turn away from them, and then turn to look at them once more. Consequently we notice the stability of some nature or entity, and we say that the thing is identical with itself. In other words, we say that something was present in our understanding in the way it is now.

123. We see of course that the reality of corporeal things is constantly changing; it varies from one moment to another. But if identity is not to be found in material things, where is it to be found? — It must be found in *ideas*, in ideal things, and hence in the faculty of apprehension where ideas are faithfully preserved. The perpetual changes registered in real and material things mean that they simply furnish us with new images and forms of concepts. Our faculty of apprehension and mental conception re-copies[88] at every moment whatever it sees, and places it amongst all the other quasi-portraits which it preserves. The changes in material things are not therefore communicated to ideas, but increase the number of ideas, all of which remain constant in their being even when corporeal things change, pass away and cease to be.

88 We think it is possible to use metaphorical language after having expounded in appropriate words our thoughts on ideas. The reader already knows the value we place on such expressions.

124. Reflection, therefore, in turning back frequently to our ideas, notices their constancy and immutability, and formulates the principle of the *identity of things*, as it is called. This means that no essence expressed in an idea is confused with any other, and that in each instant things can have only a single form. As a result, they cannot be represented in the mind by two different types, but only by one, perfectly constant type. This leads us to affirm that things are all true through themselves. We mean that they conform to a single, ideal type, incorruptible and immutable by nature.

125. The origin of the principle of the identity of things thus explains why human beings all possess this principle; we simply cannot form any concept at variance with it. Different types or essences are so distinct from one another that it is impossible for one ever to be confused with another, or taken for another. Our faculty of judgment cannot therefore be ignorant of their distinction and separation, nor of the constancy of each in its own form. Essences, because they are *simple*, would be quite different if the smallest variety were present.[89]

The same necessity is not present in our judgment, however, when we wrongly affirm or deny that a thing possesses some property which, when added to or subtracted from the thing, does not destroy it. But this occurs only and whenever our judgment is concerned with real things. In this case, the judgment can be false or correct. In other words, it can attach a predicate to something which has no claim to the predicate, or remove a predicate from something to which the predicate pertains.

126. The closest union between the real, necessary order and the moral, willed order is therefore founded in the *principle of identity*, the point at which these two orders meet, as it were, and where one finishes and the other begins. It is so small a point that until now it has escaped the vision of many.

[89] Cf. *Rinnovamento della Filosofia*, bk. 3, c. 39 ss.

VI.

Promulgation of the moral law

127. As long as we are dealing with the way in which our mind comes to possess simple ideas, that is, the essences of things, we find ourselves in the field of necessity. Ideas are presented to us as external and non-interchangeable. The intellect grasps them, and delights in their quasi-divinity. But there comes a time when we turn in on ourselves and think about the intellectual lights we have received. We ask ourselves if various properties have to be distinguished from one another in the lights we behold, or if relationships are to be found between these lights. More insistently we ask whether these relationships must be found between the lights and the things the lights make known. At this point, error can creep in.

128. Up to this moment, we have sensed things as a whole. Now we have to analyse this whole and advert to that which was first known without being adverted to. We now have to form judgments for ourselves not about the whole, but about its parts, or about the individual aspects of the whole which we feel and know. The moral order and freedom begin here; it is here that we can surrender to the attraction of the senses by judging wrongly in accordance with their inclinations, or remain above their seductions by affirming to ourselves what is true, reaching right conclusions, and assenting to whatever our unspoilt faculty of knowledge first suggested to us.

129. Only *simplicity* is necessary for us to judge uprightly. It is simplicity, stripped of all bias, that abandons itself to the truth which as it were comes to meet us. But in order to judge wrongly, it is absolutely necessary for us to contradict nature, to act *artfully* and violently. In order to be good, we need only to be passive as it were before what is true, and follow nature; to be evil, it is necessary to set in motion that sad activity which brings us into collision with what is true, that is, with something within us which remains unmoved and of itself impregnable.

130. We can conclude, therefore, that with the simple presentation of an object to our mind, the eternal law of justice is proclaimed in us. As soon as we know the object and begin to reflect upon it, we are immediately conscious of the need to

possess it as it is by acknowledging and judging it as such. There is no doubt that the unchangeableness of the essence that represents the thing to us has a kind of eternal force and absolute necessity inherent in its own simple nature. We feel that we have no power over this essence, which is what it is independently of us. If we affirm the contrary, we err inevitably and act evilly by hating the nature of the thing and the truth. We are to blame, therefore, for an intrinsically false action. Cicero was well aware of this when he wrote:

> If we have learned anything at all about philosophy, we must have a firm, deep conviction that, even if we were able to hide what we do from all the gods and from all mankind, we should nevertheless abstain from all avarice, injustice, lust and intemperance.[90]

131. The first law, therefore, is made by the *being itself of things*, independently of us, and is promulgated by the simple presence of beings to our understanding. In presenting themselves to us, they show us that it is not within our power to destroy, change or alter them in accordance with what is useful or pleasurable to us. We are indeed free to adapt ourselves or not to the entity of things, but if we attempt to alter this entity to what we wish to see, we immediately feel that we are acting falsely and deficiently. We feel that we are the *authors of evil.*

VII.

The subjective necessity of the moral law

132. Moral evil is reduced, therefore, to defective action in our will which prevents the will from attaining the term for which it was made, that is, the entity of things according to their truth. The will, which is indeed made to direct the soul to adhere to the entity known by the intellect, does not guide the soul to its term. The result is evil, defect, privation; the spirit remains cut off from the entity whose contact would bring it to perfection. The evil of the will is the evil of the spirit and of the whole soul.

90 *De Officiis*, 3: 8.

D

133. We have to understand that evil in the will is personal evil. The person resides in the will as the supreme active principle in an intelligent spirit, the principle to which all other powers are joined and to which they are subject.[91] This enables us to understand better still the nature of 'moral obligation, moral necessity'.

134. The reason why 'moral obligation' is so difficult to understand lies in our concept of necessity as 'the impossibility of doing the contrary'. We call 'necessary' anything whose contrary is logically absurd. In the same way we understand physical necessity as a real force which we are unable to conquer and overcome. But in applying the word 'necessity' to free actions, we no longer know the sense in which to take it because we no longer find any real force to necessitate action. On the contrary, morality in an action requires that the action lie within the power of freedom or the power of the will, and that it may be done in some way or other without compulsion. In this case, how can there be *necessity* in moral actions? What does the expression *moral necessity* mean? This is the difficulty that faces us in understanding the concept.

135. We begin our answer by noting that the expression certainly refers in the first instant to necessity originating from moral laws, not from physical forces. In the moral order, obligation comes from moral, not physical laws. But moral laws constrain quite differently and independently of the constraint placed by physical laws. If we succeed in describing the nature of moral constraint, therefore, we shall have solved our problem.

136. We maintain that as *physical necessity* is found in the order of reality, so *logical necessity* is found in the *ideal* order, and *moral necessity* in the order of *morality*. Physical necessity is essential to the order of real things; take away *necessity* from real things and you will no longer be able to conceive any real being. Logical necessity is essential to the order of ideas; take away *necessity* from ideas, and no idea will exist. Moral necessity is essential to the order of moral things; take away their *necessity*, and moral being is rendered impossible.

137. If the moral order is necessary, therefore, it must possess its own necessity, just as the ideal order and the real order must

[91] Cf. *AMS*, 832 ss., where the highly important teaching on human *personship* is developed.

have their ideal and real necessity if they are to be necessary. But ontology shows that being is necessary, and that it is necessary in all these three primordial forms, that is, in its real, ideal and moral form. It cannot be in one or two of the forms unless it exists in all three. Moral necessity is the same, therefore, as the necessity of being, and originates in the *intrinsic*, essential *order* of *being itself*. But let us try to explain simply the nature of this moral necessity.

138. Moral necessity is 'the necessity according to which *persons* must act in a given way in order not to render themselves defective.' This necessity does not depend on physical necessity, therefore, but exists without it. Persons can act *physically* in one of two ways, but not in one of them without losing their *personal perfection*. If these persons wish to preserve or increase their own proper perfection, they are *necessitated*, and have to act in a determined way. If they do not follow this course of action, they lose something of their dignity, their integrity and their being. And their evil consists precisely in this loss.

This is the source of moral obligation. Obligation is simply the kind of necessity which requires action in one way rather than another if the loss of personal dignity, that is, of the good proper to the person, is to be avoided.

139. It may be objected that personal good and evil are only some kind of subjective good and evil. If so, they are not in any way absolute good and evil. I have already shown,[92] however, that moral good is the point where subjective and objective good come into contact, embrace and intermingle as one.

It is indeed true that moral good and moral evil is personal good and evil, and that persons are subjects. From this point of view, personal good and evil are certainly subjective. Persons, however, are a special kind of subject. Consequently, it is not enough for this good to be subjective if it is to be moral; it must also be *personal*. So we ask: what kind of subject is the person?

140. We define person as an intelligent subject, that is, a subject of such a nature that its good consists in adhering to objective entity taken in its fullness, and therefore in its order. The good proper to the human person does not originate therefore from

[92] *SP*, bk. 4, c. 6.

the human person. Rather, persons find it in the *object* to which they unite themselves by means of a willed act of intelligence. This fact takes persons outside themselves in order to find the object which when found provides their perfection. The act of bringing persons to perfection is simply their sharing in the goodness of the object, their coupling with being.

141. What is this object? What is being? It is everything present in the idea, in the truth, in entity taken in all its extension, in eternal, impassible, divine being, full of beauty.

142. But how can persons be obliged to adhere to this object if they wish to be perfect? Does this necessity, to which they are subject, arise from the laws of their subjective nature? Yes, this necessity also has a relationship with the laws of their subjective nature. Nevertheless, this necessity is not formed by the laws of subjective-contingent nature, but rather forms and constitutes these laws. It is not the human person who produces the object; it is rather the object which produces the human person and which therefore imposes its laws on persons in the act by which they are formed.

This is a difficult concept, I admit, but persuasion of its truth is possible through profound meditation on the whole of the teaching we have so often formulated.

143. Let me try to express myself in another way. 'Person' is the power for affirming the whole of being (this involves sharing and delighting in being) as and to the extent that it has been apprehended intellectually by person. The necessity for doing this is imposed upon persons by the nature of being, not by themselves. When they see being, persons also see that it is immutable, identical with itself, and so on. They also see and feel that to say otherwise would be a *falsehood*. Falsehood, intrinsic disorder, and evident evil are synonymous. The nature of objective being, therefore, gives rise to the necessity of the acknowledgement of being by persons. Acting otherwise, persons incur their own degradation and the personal, moral evil that is its consequence.

SECTION TWO

OUR SYSTEM COMPARED WITH THE MOST NOTED SYSTEMS

144. The practical acknowledgement of being is, therefore, in my opinion, the principle of moral duties. This principle will be clearer if we compare and highlight the differences between it and principles proposed by other authors.

I.

The principle of physical necessity

145. Spinoza posited the ineluctable necessity of nature as the supreme principle of what he calls natural law. But we have seen that evil and good is called moral only in relationship to a free agent producing evil and good. If freedom is excluded, all morality, duty, right is severed at its root. Spinoza says:

> By natural law and statute I mean only the rules of nature governing each individual. According to these rules we conceive individuals as naturally determined to exist and act in a definite way. — The law governing the whole of human nature states that no one should omit anything he judges good, except with the hope of a greater good, or for fear of greater harm; no one should prefer an evil except for avoiding a greater evil or obtaining a greater good.[93]

[93] *Tract. Theol. Polit.*, c. 16. — Spinoza's moral teaching is as old as evil in the world. In the 10th. century, Mahdi Obeid Allah rebelled against Mohammed, forming his own sect. 'The universe,' he said, 'existed from eternity but has undergone a thousand different changes. There is nothing stable in the world; all beings are continually changing their form. The only goal for human beings is to enjoy life; only their own energies can limit the joys to which they aspire.' This is a compendium of Spinoza's natural law.

I have shown however that the first law imposed on the human being by the object to which his personship is ordered is not that of his subjective good or evil, but that of necessarily assenting to truth independently of any other subjective good or evil. The necessity intimated to the human being of acknowledging the truth is independent of him; it is a force that obligates from outside himself and consists in the immutability of essences. Essences do not change simply because of the help they can afford the human being; they are what they are through an eternal necessity, upon which human good and evil has no influence whatsoever. It is true that we obtain harmony and peace by freely adapting ourselves to and delighting in truth, as though it were a special friend. It is also true that in failing to acknowledge or love truth, we find ourselves at odds with ourselves and with truth. But this echo of good or evil is the effect of our having followed, or not followed, the prior, obligating force; if we do not obey this force, it threatens perpetual unrest.

146. The force, therefore, of the moral law obliging the personal human will precedes good and evil without depending on them, even though the good and evil of the subject is related to and dependent upon this force. We possess *good* by following what we previously knew *had* to be followed. The same knowledge which first revealed the obligation, reveals the fault we have committed after violating the obligation: the knowledge promulgating the law is precisely that which sanctions it. Spinoza did not sufficiently distinguish these two things, and took the second act of *sanction* to be the first act of *promulgation*. Consequently, he and others affirmed that human beings are naturally determined to follow always what appears to them as the greater good. But we have seen that although we are determined relative to our faculty of apprehension, we are not determined relative to the faculty by which we judge the value of the entity of the thing we have apprehended.

147. Confusing these two faculties was Spinoza's first error and led him directly to deprive human beings of their freedom to give or withhold their assent to the truth, which was his second error. He saw only one principle of human actions: their apparent utility. But there are two principles: one's own utility and the force of truth and justice.

[146–147]

II.

The principles of pleasure, utility and happiness

148. Similar to Spinoza's principle is that of Epicurus, who made *pleasure* the supreme principle of human actions. But nothing cleverly thought or said to justify this principle frees it from the force of the objections against Spinoza's principle.

I have said that we feel pleasure when we follow the truth. But the question consists in knowing whether *pleasure* is the *object* to which we must direct our attention when acting. Pleasure, whether corporal or spiritual, is always something relative to us; *truth*, as we have already pointed out, demands our assent with a force totally independent of ourselves. This force is eternal, proper to truth itself, and we in our insignificance are nothing compared with it. We cannot change anything in it, no matter how much pain or pleasure urges us to do so. We can know what is painful, but things do not cease to be true simply because they are painful, nor do they diminish our obligation to acknowledge them for what they are. Troublesome things can indeed cause us pain in so far as they are troublesome; at the same time they give us a certain peace in so far as they are fully acknowledged by us as true. To put it briefly, we feel an obligation to acknowledge them not because individually or collectively they bring us peace, but because each carries the message: 'I am true. Behold me, and acknowledge me.'

149. It is self-evident that we must follow good, but we cannot therefore conclude that we must follow subjective good. The proposition is true only when it refers to good in itself, that is, it is the nature of the apprehended object which obliges human beings, not their own pleasure or utility. Explained in this way, the teaching that 'human beings must follow good' is no different from my own teaching, because all natures are good in so far as they are conceivable.

150. The principle which Burlamachi and others re-elaborated and re-presented is ultimately that of happiness. It was defended in two ways: either 1. by saying that happiness and the supreme good are the same, or 2. by appealing to the instinct of human

nature, which amounts to the same thing.[94] In answer to the first of these explanations, I say that what is good in itself is indeed our good. But must we follow it because it is good in itself, or because it is our good? — the whole problem lies here.

The obligation originates from the object in such a way that even relative to those for whom the truth is the greatest torment, that is, for the devils in hell, there is an equal obligation to respect and love it; these condemned spirits are tormented precisely by the ceaseless force of this obligation.

151. Instinct certainly moves us, but it does not *oblige* us to move. Sometimes it will direct us to carrying out what we are in any case obliged to do. But even if it opposed the carrying out of our obligation, we would still remain obliged. The obligation therefore does not depend on our inclination or aversion to carrying out the obligation. Finally, an upright instinct can certainly make the Creator's will known to us when we consider the instinct as coming from him and as a sign of the end he has put before all his creatures. Here instinct is simply an *indication* for discovering the source of the obligation and cannot constitute the obligation itself.

152. When Carneades tried to demonstrate that justice did not exist, he took as the basis of his seductive reasoning the

[94] Aware of the weakness of the principle of *utility*, many authors have turned to *instinct* but failed to notice that they have not changed the principle, only the way of demonstrating it. In the first case, utility is sought as a result of counsel from reason; in the second, as a result of the inclination of nature. If *utility* were to be a good foundation for justice, following it by *reason* would certainly be more worthy than following it by blind *instinct*. Buchanan is one of these authors, cf. his Dialogue, *De iure regni apud Scotos*. In the dialogue he objects that his opponent had proposed utility as the first and supreme conciliator among human beings: 'If somebody wants an explanation for his own utility, don't you see that utility would divide rather than unite society?' His opponent replies; 'That is perhaps true. But I would like to know what other source there is of human fellowship.' Buchanan answers: 'The other source is a certain power of nature present not only in human beings but in the more gentle of other animals. Even if the blandishments of utility were absent, they would freely associate with animals of the same kind, etc.' But the origin of this inclination of animals to associate with others of the same kind can only be the pleasure they experience. The inclination arises therefore from some good or utility of their own which they draw from the association although, because instinct is blind, they do not know this.

argument that if justice existed, its principle would have to be utility. Granted this, he was certain his argument could not be refuted. It ran as follows: the principle of justice is constituted either by our own or by another's utility. If it is our own, we are simply aware of acting for our own advantage. If it is another's, we are simply acting stupidly, because we would often harm ourselves by helping others, and would foolishly put another's utility before our own![95]

III.

The principle of sociality

153. Fiorentino, Grotius and others deduced human duties from *sociality*, as did Cicero, although not exclusively.[96] This

[95] *Carneadis summa disputationis haec fuit: Jura sibi homines pro utilitate sanxisse, scilicet varia pro moribus, et apud eosdem pro temporibus saepe mutata; jus autem naturale esse nullum. Omnes et homines et alias animantes ad utilitates suas natura ducente ferri; proinde aut nullum esse justitiam, aut si sit aliqua, summam esse stultitiam, quoniam sibi noceret alienis commodis consulens* (Lactantius, bk. 5, c. 16). — It is noticeable how the word 'nature', granted its many meanings, is always open to sophistry. One of the false arguments used by Carneades, as we can see in Cicero (*De Rep.*, 3: 11), to annihilate natural law rested upon the opinion that nature is constant and does not manifest variety. It is indeed true that nature is constant, if by nature we mean the *essences* of things, but not true if we mean subsistent things themselves. These are forever changing and altering, disintegrating and renewing themselves.

[96] 'One single thing must therefore be proposed for everybody so that utility is the same for all. If anyone should appropriate utility to himself, all human association would be terminated. Even if nature prescribes that one human being provide for another, whoever he may be, it is still necessary, according to nature itself, that the utility of all be common, precisely because other persons are human beings' (*De Offic.*, 3: 2). We notice here how much Cicero is aware of the truth. He sees that the *human being* as such must be considered, not just the *citizen*. But in place of considering the benefit and harm one human being can do to another, Cicero should have considered the respect of mind and heart due to human nature even when neither good nor evil can be done to human nature, and the respect due is unknown to the recipient. If he had done this, Cicero would have come very near the

principle can be understood in two ways: either as the *instinct* which human beings have for associating with their like, or as a *calculation* of reason by which they understand they can obtain their own individual utility by promoting the common utility. — Both cases are reduced to the principle of *utility*; the principle of *righteousness* is not attained. The difference between the two cases is that instinct directs us to what is useful by a movement that necessarily impels us and cannot properly speaking be called self-interested; reasoning directs us to what is useful by means of conscious deliberation, which can rightly be called self-interested.

We should not be surprised therefore if, as an ancient author observed,[97] Cicero was thrown off balance by Carneades' arguments against justice. He tried to end the dispute by saying very unphilosophically (although he may have thought it a pleasantry) that he would rather placate his opponent with kind words than provoke him to argue.[98] If we grant that human beings must follow what is useful, then there is no longer any reason why we should place another's usefulness before our own, or, in cases of conflict, place what is useful to the group before what is useful to us individually. When the only value of social usefulness is what is useful to oneself, the former is a means, and the latter an end. These authors, however, led by a naturally upright feeling, sometimes admit that what is just can be distinguished by means of its own immutable nature from what is unjust, although they cannot fully define that nature.[99]

essence of morality.

[97] 'These subtle points were as deadly as poison, and Marcus Tullius could not refute them. When he made Laelius reply to Furius in favour of justice, he passed over these unrefuted points as a trap. Consequently it seemed as if Laelius himself defended not natural justice, which had been judged stupidity, but civil justice, which Furius had accepted as wisdom, although unjust wisdom' (Lactantius, bk. 5, c. 17).

[98] Speaking in Book 1 of *Laws* about the opinions of the latest Academy on justice, he does not dare refute them, but prefers to pass them over in silence. 'Let us say nothing about all those things dealt with in this latest disturbing Academy held by Arcessila and Carneades. There will be real trouble, if the Academy attacks the reasons which to us seem assembled and ordered wisely enough. I want to pacify the Academy; I dare not refute it.'

[99] There cannot be any more splendid eulogy in antiquity in praise of the immutable law of justice than in those lines of Cicero reported by Lactantius

[153]

IV.

The principles of fear and force

154. 'We must admit that laws were established for fear of what is unjust.'[100] According to Hobbes this ancient statement affirms that human beings associated in order to find protection against mutual harm. This is true to a certain extent, but it does not explain the origin of duties and rights. How could mutual agreement be valid if the law of justice did not previously exist? Utility alone, and in particular the fear of evil, does not impart force to an agreement. This kind of restriction is insufficient for the powerful who have nothing to fear from the weak.

Hobbes' system, as generally understood, is one of the many forms of the utilitarianism I have already refuted. It is also vitiated by the error claiming that, before the formation of society, a natural, absolute human right to everything existed for all. This error is compounded in turn by the claim that it is deduced from the equally erroneous principle that duty, moral law and valid possession did not exist before the formation of society!

155. In antiquity people like Plato's Trasimachus placed every right in force. Hobbes allied himself with them. — Force can constitute a fact but never a right. If violated right is what forms fault, and if force can be overcome only by a greater force, right

(*Instit.* 6: 8). In Lactantius' opinion they express the law of God as if the divine voice had spoken: 'Right reason in harmony with nature is real, constant and eternal law, diffused in all of us. It urges duty by command; it deters from falsity by prohibition. It does not vainly command or forbid decent people, or by command or prohibition dissuade evil people. Such a law cannot be obrogated or derogated in part, nor can it be totally abrogated. Neither the Senate nor the people can excuse us from this law, nor is its interpretation or explanation to be sought from any human being. There is not one law for Rome and another for Athens, nor one law now and another later. There is one, immutable, eternal law embracing all peoples and all times. The God of all is its one, common teacher and ruler; he is the founder, arbitrator and proposer of this law. Anyone who will not obey it will flee, but having despised human nature will undergo the greatest punishments even if he escapes all other troubles.'

[100] Horat., bk. 1, Sat. 3.

(force) in this case would be violated by a greater right (by a greater force); no right would ever be violated.

Force simply indicates necessity. Right and duty include in their notion free will, which can execute right and duty or not.

Finally Hobbes is led by his absurd principles to justify tyranny as that which alone can prevent universal violence. In his view human beings will always be mutually violent unless someone exists who can accomplish all things.

V.

The principle of common will

156. Others have proposed common will as the principle of duties and of human rights. But who will oblige me to submit if I do not wish to do so? I need a preceding law that tells me I am obliged to consent to the will of others. If the common good is indicated in place of law, we return to the system of sociality or utility that we have examined.

VI.

The principle of the will of a superior

157. Pufendorf and others who posited the principle of justice in the will of a superior were also wide of the mark. As Leibniz noted, this view does not determine whether such a will is blind and arbitrary, or guided by wisdom. Pufendorf, who confined the end of natural right to the present life, was aware that if we admitted the principle of right solely in the decree of a superior, there would be no duty if there were no superior. Thus, in nations which lacked a common head, natural law would be destroyed. As a remedy and antidote for this erroneous doctrine, he had to introduce the divinity surreptitiously. Leibniz justifiably was not satisfied:

> We cannot, as Grotius carefully noted, pass over in silence the fact that some natural obligation must be present, granted even that God did not exist or were set aside as if he did not exist. — We must bear in mind that God praises himself because he is just. There is a certain kind of justice, or rather a supreme justice in God, although he has no superior, and through the spontaneity of his surpassing nature excels in everything that he does, so that no one can reproach him.[101]

VII.

The principle of charity in a wise person

158. Considerations like these led Leibniz to place the principle of morality in the wisdom of a totally good nature and to define justice as 'charity in a wise person'.

> I do not know whether, after so many outstanding authors, we have the notions of *right* and *justice* sufficiently clear. Right is a moral power; obligation a moral necessity. By 'moral' I understand the same as 'natural' in a good human being. The Roman lawyer says so well that we must believe we are quite *unable* to do anything contrary to good behaviour. Furthermore, the good human being is the one who loves all human beings to the extent indicated by reason. Justice, therefore, which is the controlling virtue of the affection the Greeks call φιλανθρωπιαν, can fittingly be defined (if I am not deceived) as charity in the wise person, that is, charity which follows the dictates of wisdom.[102]

The search for the principle by which justice springs up in human beings has passed from the force of nature to the force of instinct; from instinct to common utility; from utility to

[101] *Monita quaedam ad Samuelis Pufendorfii principia*, §4.

[102] *Dissertatio de Actorum publicorum usu, atque de principiis Juris naturae et Gentium*, §11. The passage is found at the beginning of Part 1 of the *Cod. Diplom. delle Genti etc.*

common will; from common will to force and the will of a superior, and from the arbitrary will of a superior to the wise will of a benevolent human being.

159. This last idea of Leibniz is certainly nearest the truth. This admirable man would surely have perfected his noble thought if he had gone on from wisdom to the very objects of wisdom, that is, to the nature of things, which demands acknowledgement and respect from our minds. He did not take this step, and consequently his teaching remains doubtful. By saying that justice 'is the virtue which orders benevolence according to the dictates of wisdom,' he leaves himself open to the criticism that his definition is a vicious circle because it is justice itself that indicates what wisdom must suggest to benevolence. Thus, the definition becomes: 'Justice is the virtue which directs benevolence according to the dictates of justice'.

It is true that he defines wisdom as the 'knowledge of happiness'. But we can ask whether this happiness must be understood in accordance with the dictates of justice and as an effect of justice. If not, we fall back into the system of utility. Nor can it be said that the greatest happiness is justice itself. If we imagined that in the just human being there had to be enough wisdom to calculate the greatest happiness obtainable in the universe, nobody could ever be just without infinite wisdom. On the contrary we could be certain of deceiving ourselves when calculating the happiness we obtain both for ourselves and for others. Following such a system we could in fact convince ourselves of acting according to the norm of the science of happiness in performing an unjust act to save a multitude of unfortunate people from disaster.

160. Leibniz cannot deny this supposition if he wishes to be coherent with his principles. According to the system that he laid down with great ingenuity in his *Theodicy*, nothing happens except for the greatest good, the greatest happiness of intelligent beings. It is therefore impossible for human beings ever to act contrary to the science of universal happiness. If they had to follow this science alone and possessed infinite wisdom, they would act according to the principles of Leibniz's theodicy, as they do at the moment, whether they act justly or unjustly. In the great calculation their acts would be part of the totally good order of the universe. In the vision of wisdom, which shows

how maximum happiness is to be established in the universe, even their mistakes and perversities would be necessary.

161. For us to be just therefore it is not sufficient that our benevolence be guided by knowledge of happiness; it must properly be guided by the science of *justice*, which is essentially different from *happiness*. If I wish to attain the science of happiness, I have to know an infinite number of things. On the other hand the science of justice is simple, and I acquire it when things are presented to me for the first time. It does not come to birth with science but with truth, and begins by commanding me to acknowledge truth as soon as the latter shines on me.

VIII.

The principle of universal benevolence

162. Richard Cumberland is very close to Leibniz in establishing the supreme principle of morality. Like Leibniz he locates the principle

> in universal benevolence accompanied by a certain sagacity which always directs benevolence to the good of the whole rather than of a part.

He establishes what is just and upright when he writes:

> The effort we make, in so far as possible, for the common good, that is, for the good of the whole system of rational agents, leads, as far as we are concerned, to the good of the individual parts in which our happiness lies, as people who are part of the whole. Acts which are the opposite of this effort bring with them, amongst other evils, our own misery.[103]

163. The objections I made against Leibniz apply here also. For example, it is incorrect to suppose that justice depends on such an extensive wisdom. On the contrary justice is necessarily present in every human being in whom the tiniest ray of reason

[103] In the prolegomena of *De Legibus naturae*, etc., §9.

shines. The force of obligation reveals itself in us in the very act by which from our first moment the force of truth reveals itself to us. Although we may know only one intelligent object and be ignorant of its relationship with all that co-exists with it in the universe, its presence alone would inform us when we turn our attention to it, that we must acknowledge it for the intelligent being it is, and because of its worth, respect and love it.

The nature of justice therefore is simpler than these thinkers make it. It must be so if its light is to shine equally in all human beings.

IX.

The principles of objective order, appropriateness and beauty

164. The great scholar Gerdil, following St. Augustine, proposed the doctrine of *order*. But not even this doctrine can entirely satisfy us in our search for the *supreme* principle of natural probity.[104] Although order can help greatly in deducing duties and rights, it does not attain that ultimate point where all duties begin. The doctrine states: 'In all our actions we must preserve the natural relationships of appropriateness which exist among things.' We certainly cannot deny this, but such a doctrine presupposes that we know many things and see their relationships. As we have seen, however, the law of justice is simpler, and its truth shines in our mind as soon as the first object appears. And if we know many things we must preserve their relationships. But what are our duties to each individual thing, considered in itself and abstracted from all other things?

165. The first of all relationships, if we wish to keep this word 'relationship', is clearly the IDENTITY OF THINGS, as we have already explained. However, each thing is truly one, and

[104] Cf. the article, *Principes métaphysiques de la Morale chrétienne*, and the dissertation, *Sull' origine del senso morale*, in the works of Cardinal Gerdil, vol. 2, Roman edition.

relationship can exist only between two different things. Hence, the statement that the law reveals itself to us by relationships is not very exact, although it is quite exact to say, as we have said, that the law is presented to us by the essences of things.

166. *Beauty*, which Plato frequently ascribes to virtue, and *appropriateness* between things, to which the Stoics assigned probity, do not greatly differ from the doctrine of Sigismund Gerdil.

X.

The principle of order in the divine mind

167. Vico also took from St. Augustine a similar doctrine and presented it in his book, *Del principio e fine unico di ogni diritto* [The unique principle and end of every right]. According to him, however, we must begin with the concept of order, and from there ascend to the demonstration of the existence of an infinite mind, author of eternal truths. From this vantage point the notion of natural probity could be deduced. Vico posited this notion in the contemplation and love of the perfect, infinite Being, in whom the eternal truths are contained. Thus he had found the apex to which human virtue could attain, but had missed its origin.

168. I have observed that knowledge of many things is not necessary. Nor do they need to be resplendent and excellent for the force of some moral duty to be revealed to us. It is sufficient that we perceive a single intelligent object. And in the *first stages* of natural justice, knowledge of an infinite, subsistent being is not necessary. This kind of knowledge is certainly necessary when we consider justice attaining perfection. *Supernatural justice*, however, begins only with the feeling or apprehension of God.

169. Vico's argument is further weakened because he thought it necessary to deduce an eternal truth from an eternal order of things. But because truth precedes order, he should have deduced eternal order, which is multiple, from eternal truth, which

is simple.[105] We must not confuse our ideas here by saying that because truth is the order existing between what is known and the knowing mind, therefore truth is an order. We are not discussing the order between a thing and the mind. This order cannot be the object of the mind unless we presuppose that the mind, through a renewed reflection on itself and on the thing it knows, begins to contemplate such a relationship. Finally, Vico erred by passing rather ambitiously from abstract truth (an ideal entity) to subsisting things.

170. We must also take note of the greater evidence and of the infallibility of the principle of *practical acknowledgement* compared with the principle of *order* and the principle of the *common good.*

Error can always be committed in calculating the common good or in examining the order of things. But we cannot err in sensing the degree of being which things have. There may be lack of clarity in the *consequences* of morality, but there can be none in the *principle*. The moral principle can be founded only in natural, evident apprehension, not in some obscure calculation. The utility and certainty of experience, which the sciences recommend so much, can only arise if they deal with one thing at a time. Ordinary people themselves first follow securely the sure way of experience of individual things. Only then do they unite the single truths they have ascertained. In this way people as a whole make great progress without being aware of it, as they form new languages and change old. Languages, which have their own stable and universal laws, provide distinctions in ideas and subtleties of logic that even the wise marvel at. We should in fact consider languages as the deposit of the wisdom of nations.

This great mass of distinct ideas and cognitions, so well bound together, was not deduced however from some previous, great system; it moved forward step by step, giving special meaning to the least thing presented to thought. Thus, bit by bit, by

[105] Cf. his book, *De uno universi juris principio etc.*, where he says: 'The eternal order of things demonstrates eternal truth.' He should in fact have said the opposite, because it is evident that logically the notion of what is true precedes the notion of order. His demonstration of the existence of God, however, is placed at the beginning of the book.

faithfully noting the individual parts, people finally gathered a huge stock of harmoniously joined signs. Portraying abstract ideas, things or human feelings and actions faithfully at the time they present themselves, and indicating them with a word, syllable or other sign is a kind of justice exercised towards these things. In the same way individual human beings learn their duties and discover moral norms one by one. And so, moral knowledge, impoverished at first and almost invisible, but finally rich and co-ordinated in a wonderful system, is gradually developed in them.

XI.

The principle of self-perfection in general

171. The principle, 'Be perfect', can under a certain aspect be classified with those principles which make utility the norm for human beings. It is true that the supporters of these systems claim not to exclude virtue but to enjoin it strictly as the only or principal *means* of human perfection. However, when they grant virtue the quality of being a means of human perfection and happiness, they inadvertently concede that their notion of *virtue* differs from that of happiness and *perfection*. They argue that the idea of virtue is in a class of its own, and cannot be confused in any way with other ideas of utility, happiness and perfection; it has its own existence and nature, independent of those notions.

172. The moral question is therefore reduced to knowing the elements that form the essence of virtue. All our thinkers reason about virtue, presuppose it, and in fact admit that they would prefer it to exist — provided it did not command. They should therefore first enlighten us in simple terms about the force that imposes an obligation on us, and makes those practising or rejecting it praiseworthy or blameable? Sidestepping the question or speaking about virtue and duty as if they were obvious is no answer — in the first place we want to know what these things are, and then be told whether virtue produces perfection

or not. To apportion praise and blame according to virtue and never according to happiness is certainly good. But in this case virtue must have its own power to draw praise from human beings, independently of happiness and almost in opposition to it. A virtuous person appears more sublime in misfortune, and consequently requires greater admiration.

173. As I said, all this can be applied to the principle of perfection under one aspect; another aspect strengthens the argument. If we are required to tend to our own *perfection*, we must implicitly propose some good for ourselves. This good, although perhaps not absolute, is connected with absolute good as an effect with its cause. However, because we do not see the connection too easily, the principle remains obscure.

174. Some people object that we can act only through the principle of self-perfection. If this is true, the principle of perfection cannot be the moral principle, which must leave us free, binding us only morally. It is true that the tendency to fulfil our own existence and satisfaction is certainly mixed with the most disinterested, objective actions, but this does not make the tendency a moral principle.

What makes us use our reflection for the sake of knowing through judgment the value, dignity, and excellence of a being perceived by us? Why don't we remain inactive and indifferent without judging the being? The fact is that a natural inclination to self-fulfilment and perfection spurs us to use our faculties to overcome our inertia whatever the cost to ourselves.

175. Let us grant therefore that our human instinct for perfection draws us into action. However, while attributing to instinct everything that belongs to it, we must be careful not to exaggerate its *power*, which urges us to action rather than inaction, but nothing more. On the other hand the *law* about following truth and virtue obligates us not simply to action but to a certain *mode* of action, that is, to right and virtuous action. It is precisely here that the instinct for perfection, an intrinsic principle of human nature, is entirely different from the moral principle.

Instinct is a power, a reality; the moral principle is a law, ideality. The former makes us act, the latter directs our manner of acting. The instinct for perfection leads us to reflect on things perceived; the demands of truth authoritatively require us to acknowledge reflectively things perceived for what they actually are, without suspending our assent to the intellectual and practical esteem due to their endowments. Thus, while it is true that we naturally act with a tendency to good, it is equally true that we are obliged to act according the law of truth and justice that stands clearly before us. Truth's urging is simple and free of all human interest; it is we who intermingle the voice of our own inclinations and interests with the voice of eternal, impassible truth, and replace the latter with the former.

176. The *being* of actions therefore arises from the tendency to perfection, but the *manner* of their being *must* arise from the principle of justice. We are not obliged to act by nature — it is instinct that causes action. But when we do act, we are obliged by the moral force of *justice* to act correctly.[106]

177. It may still be objected that because we are bound by the

[106] When I say that we are not obliged to act, I refer to our first reflections, the actions through which nature itself begins our development. These are not the result of any obligation (because we know of no obligation) but of the physical sensations we experience and of natural instincts. Any actions to which we are morally *obliged* can be understood according to the following formula which determines our *manner* of acting in general: 'Act in *such a way* as to offend no one.' This formula applies to the *manner* of acting as a whole, not to individual actions. But for the *manner* of all human actions as *a whole* to be correct, some must be posited and others omitted; thus the obligation to act arises indirectly.

There are, however, innumerable other human actions which, because of their moral probity, may be freely carried out.

Nevertheless, if we perform these morally free actions rightly, the number we perform is neither meaningless nor indifferent relative to happiness and morality. Such actions can greatly enrich our joy and merit: just as a person who accumulates material riches with great effort attains a higher standard of living, so others, if they labour to improve the lot of their fellows, obtain a great store of moral goodness, which results from actions spontaneously undertaken without any obligation. This is the difference between *goodness* and *justice*.

Goodness consists in seeking to make others more perfect and happy through actions done spontaneously and without obligation. Justice does not consist in doing many actions for others but in not doing any harmful action to them. Thus, *justice* determines the way of acting, *goodness* increases the number of our actions.

The reasons governing action therefore are two: first, the instinct for our own development or, as it is normally called, our perfection, which precedes the use of our freedom; and second, love for the perfection of others, a free reason, constituting our own moral perfection.

law of instinct, we must always have a subjective good before us as the term of our actions. — Even if this were true, I would say that we are nevertheless always morally obliged by the law of justice. Any good not in accord with this unalterable law must therefore be omitted. But what must we do when a decree of justice requires us to sacrifice riches, honour and life and, disregarding our pleasure or pain, declares as wrong that which is wrong, and as right that which is right? — Those who know neither God nor a future life, or know God without sufficient light and certain faith, will probably give in, overcome or terrified by pain. But an internal, relentless voice will accompany them, even to their last breath: 'By acting in this way, you offend truth.' We could indeed imagine some natural support sustaining them against such a terrible temptation and restraining them from acting wrongly, but the support comes only from some hidden feeling, some thought deep within them, offering another good beyond this present life, and greater than life itself. This indication or, as it were, this sublime proclamation hidden in their hearts would perhaps be their only lifeline in the midst of moral shipwreck.[107]

178. Hence Lactantius, speaking of the time before Christ, says: 'It was very easy at that time to subvert justice because it had no roots. Philosophers had not in fact penetrated to the nature and quality of justice.'[108]

In my opinion this explanation is correct. Before Christ,

[107] The difficulty of establishing lasting harmony between human happiness and virtue has always been experienced. Like us, the pagans also heard two voices proclaiming: 'Be happy' and 'Be just'. Some philosophers, the Stoics among them, tried to settle the question by affirming that happiness must consist in perfect virtue. In saying this they recognised that the question had two parts, thus unconsciously admitting that the notion of happiness is in fact different from that of justice. They divided the tract on moral duties into two parts, calling the first *dogmatics*, in which they intended to establish the doctrine of good and bad things, and the second, *parenetics*, in which they discussed moral duties. 'The question of duty is double-sided,' Cicero says, discussing the matter. 'One part concerns the destined end of what is good; the other, precepts, to which our pattern of life should totally conform' (*De Offic.*, bk. 1, c. 3).

[108] *Erat facillimum justitiam radicem non habentem labefactare, quia tum nulla in terra fuit, ut quid esset, aut qualis, a philosophis cerneretur* (Lactantius, bk. 5, c. 14).

justice was something abstract, not a real good. The truth of justice, because self-evident, could not be contradicted, but very often philosophers of the time found no means of reconciling it with the instinct for happiness. They saw that whatever is good in the present life could on occasion conflict with justice, but they did not have to hand a greater good which necessarily accorded with justice. So what could they do or say as long as the voice of justice was still there, speaking supremely and inflexibly? They could only confuse two contrary voices; pyrrhonism, proclaimed by those who thought themselves wise, became the universal system.

179. Lactantius says appropriately therefore:

> Carneades sensed the nature of justice, but was unable to go further and safeguard it from the taint of stupidity that arose from its sometimes promoting harm. He could not explain this, and took the opportunity of reiterating his teaching that truth was hidden, and outside the capacities of human perception.[109]

He adds:

> But we do not know justice solely by name; we know it in fact.[110]

This means we have not only the abstract *idea* of justice, as the pagans do, but also *real*, subsistent justice, justice which is not only object of the faculty of *abstraction* and a rule of life, but also object of the faculty of *thought*[111] and will, a true end for human beings; justice which is not only inflexible and eternal, but attractive and beatifying. In a word, this justice is an

[109] *Sensit igitur Carneades quae sit natura justitiae; nisi quod parum alte prospexit, stultitiam non esse; quamquam intelligere mihi videor qua mente id fecerit. Non enim existimavit eum stultum esse qui justus est; sed cum sciret non esse, et rationem tamen cur ita videretur non comprehenderet, voluit ostendere, latere in abdito veritatem, ut decretum disciplinae suae tueretur, cuius summa sententia est, nihil percipi posse* (Lactantius, bk. 5, c. 17. Cf. also the *Epitome*, c. 55).

[110] 'This defence is easier for us to whom divine condescension has really made known justice. We are familiar with it NOT BY NAME BUT IN REALITY' (Lactantius, bk. 5, c. 17).

[111] For my understanding of the *faculty of thought* as the opposite of the *faculty of abstraction* cf. *SP*, bk. 4, c. 23.

indefectible nature, a God, the ultimate aim of the appetite for happiness, as supreme good, and of the moral will, as living justice.[112] God is the centre of the whole human being who, redeemed and regenerated, can despise the vanities of the present time by fulfilling the duty of justice with the same act by which he seeks to obtain his own good.[113]

[112] We can say that the Stoics had glimpsed the nature of the matter, or rather had come to understand that justice, like truth, was inflexible, and that all the pain to which we might be subject was insufficient to justify a single offence against it. They were however a long way from discovering the real core of such a tremendous problem. To convince ourselves of this, we need only observe the false idea they had of God. God was nature itself, where everything was continually intermingling: 'All this in which we are contained,' says Seneca (*Lett.* 94), 'is one and is God; we are his companions and members.' Sometimes they said that justice comes from God but, in their understanding, this God was human reason or the common nature of things (cf. Plutarch). They distinguished two responsibilities or duties, the *perfect* and the *common* or *average* (Cic. *De Offic.*, bk. 1, c. 4). People who followed *perfect duty* were wise, close to the gods; they were God. They experienced no disturbance or unhappiness. Those who followed *average or common* responsibility were decent people, who practised political and moral virtues. The first lived above nature and were called *theoreticians*; the second lived in conformity with nature and were called *practitioners*. Because the second were only proficients, they suffered distress; in them justice was not perfectly united with happiness.

Despite these fine words, the Stoics were nevertheless aware of the weak condition of humanity, and debated whether a perfect person, forever blessed by justice, could really be found on earth. Seneca thought so (*De Const. Sap.*, c. 7) but compared such a person to the phoenix: 'Perhaps like the Phoenix, such a person is born once in 500 years' (*Letter*. 42). Stoic pride however affected this just and blessed wisdom, which was also hard and inflexible. Under its cover and in its name all vices were practised, although anyone who possessed such wisdom professed to be sinless. Josephus therefore rightly commented that the sect possessed characteristics similar to that of the Pharisees (in his 'Autobiography').

[113] The situation in which Carneades wished to place human beings brought them to some frightening collisions, as they saw their boast of strict justice go up in smoke. Just as the description of food does not satisfy a starving man, so the abstract idea alone of what is upright and just, with no eternal reward, does not comfort humanity in its torments. Furius, in his exposition of Carneades' argument in book 4 of the *Republica Tulliana*, says: 'Let us imagine that there are two men, one of whom is an excellent person, very fair-minded, supremely just and singularly trustworthy; the other is known for his wickedness and arrogance. Let us also imagine that the city

180. I conclude with Lactantius again: 'The explanation of justice lies in equity; its origin' (its realisation) 'in religion.'[114] Everyone is capable of seeing the reason for justice, present to every mind, but we can only reconcile it with human nature when religion indicates to our heart a subsistent justice where the rational appetite discovers the greatest good, the object of its search. Uncovering this secret, religion calms the doubting mind and reassures the fretful soul.

XII.

The principle of moral perfection

181. If however the principle of perfection is determined and restricted solely to moral perfection, it approximates to our principle of truth. *Moral perfection* does not result from a subjective way of considering ourselves but from the objects we know and acknowledge, objects which we love rightly and treat according to right love. The weakness of the principle of moral perfection is that our attention stops at the effect rather than at the essence of morality, which is what we are seeking.

182. Another weakness is that it does not include the whole of virtue but only the more perfect part of it, that is, goodness. Our principle, on the contrary, in addition to manifesting more

mistakenly thinks the good man wicked, evil, nefarious, and the dishonest man of the highest integrity and trustworthiness. Moreover, because all the citizens think alike, the good man is harassed and molested, his hands are cut off and his eyes dug out; he is condemned, bound, burnt, exterminated, impoverished, and afterwards with full justification seen by everyone as the most miserable. The wicked man, however, is praised, honoured and loved by all; all honours, dominion, riches and total abundance are conferred upon him. He is in the estimation of all a good man and judged most worthy of all good fortune. Who then would be so mad as to doubt which of the two he would prefer to be?' Leibniz, in his observations on Pufendorf, says: 'To subordinate all that is truly and irrefutably good to gaining an immortal name and posthumous fame, that is, to opinions we shall never hear, would be nothing less than glaring stupidity.'

[114] *Cuius origo in religione, ratio in aequitate est* (Lact., bk. 5, c. 14).

clearly the disinterestedness of the upright person, includes both *goodness* and *justice.* The latter is the foundation and the substance, as it were, of the former; the former is the perfection of the latter.

XIII.

The principle of the ends of things

183. The maxim, 'We must act in accordance with the ends of things', is also excellent, provided we accept it with certain reservations, and without judging it by strict scientific standards. Otherwise, it would be neither totally clear nor adequate as the supreme principle of morality. The word 'ends' itself is equivocal, because every single thing has *internal* and *external ends*, which refer to the good of the entire thing. Other defects which concern the substance and expression of the principle exclude it from the ranks of truly scientific propositions. For example, it forbids us to act against the ends of things but does not tell us whether we *must* also positively act in accordance with them, nor how extensive our activity must be in support of these ends. As a moral principle it would at least lack universality.

184. The maxim presupposes that the things with which we find ourselves in relationship have not yet obtained their end. But morality also imposes on us certain things relative to natures which have already obtained the end of their existence, or have this perfect end within them, as God does.

On the other hand, the principle I have proposed includes our duties towards all natures, perfect or not, whether they have obtained or not the end for which they were made.

XIV.

The principle of the will of the supreme Being

185. Martini[115] *adds to the* principle of the ends of things the will of the Creator which imposes the ends. The will of the Creator can either be interpreted in the ends things have, or understood as ordinary, positive will, but we cannot consider such a will as the *first* moral principle. The law or reason which is *relative to our manner of mental conception* precedes all others in the moral order. Who in fact tells me that the Creator's will is to be respected? We need a reason for respecting the will of the Creator, a reason which is antecedent (in the order of our mind) to that most holy will. What we need is the law of reason which makes me discern in general what is and is not to be respected, and discern in particular the respect due to the will of the Creator. I would obviously be going around in a circle if I said that the *obligation* incumbent upon me to respect the Creator's will arose solely from the fact that the Creator's will commands me to respect it.

186. The first law with which we judge the *exigency of things* is, in the order of our mind, different from the will of the Creator and of any superior whatsoever. Through this law I know the respect due to such a will; it is not through such a will that I know the respect due to the law. In a word, if the law is to be first, it must be immediate, promulgated in us through itself, and self-evident; nothing must judge it — it must judge everything. These characteristics are solely those of that *law of truth* which I have proposed. Truth is the light without which we cannot know beings or measure their worth. Hence in the Scriptures, *truth* is called the *principle* of the revealed law itself, *PRINCIPIUM verborum tuorum, veritas.*[116]

187. It is in the idea of *supreme being* that I find the reason for respecting it, just as in the idea of *person* I find the reason why the person should be respected. Now there is certainly an *idea*, the idea of *entity*, with which I know all beings. As soon as I

115 *De Lege naturali, positiones in usum Auditorii Vindobonensis. Viennae, Austriae,* 1767, c. 3.

116 Ps 118: [160, Douai].

consider this idea in its power to make me know the entity of particular things, and in this entity their moral exigency, the idea takes the form of light, first norm and first law. But the universal entity of all possible things leads us immediately into God.

[187]

SECTION THREE

THE RELATIONSHIP BETWEEN THE MORAL AND THE RELIGIOUS PRINCIPLE

188. The humanitarian need for religion, an intimate, supreme need, is felt by all, even by those who take great care to disguise and hide it. Before continuing therefore I must examine more carefully the nature of the relationship between *morality* (whose principle I have just posited and defended) and *religion* in order to discover whether morality is independent of religion or can benefit from it. If religion can render morality more complete, this alone is sufficient to oblige discussion amongst moralists so that they can complete and confirm in every part the moral system they are positing. Moreover, a writer on natural right must also discuss the matter, because, as we have mentioned (and shall see better later on), morality is the unshakeable foundation of the whole science of right.

I.

Can the first moral law have the form of an express command of God?

189. As I have already shown above, it would be a patent error to claim that at the first manifestation of moral obligation a Legislator *distinct* from the law must also be revealed — as though the law could not produce in us a first, truly binding obligation unless it appeared as a *positive wish* on the part of a Legislator distinct from the law. Indeed, the moral obligation which binds me to respect and obey the Legislator must necessarily be that which counsels respect and obedience to the Legislator's words and will.

190. In the system, therefore, which alone I believe conforms to the mind and tradition of the Church, the *first law* and the *Legislator* are fused; the law is a law-legislator or (if preferred) a legislator-law. As I said, only when a being is made known to

me, can I know that its will is to be respected. If I am informed that the being in question is supreme, the Author of everything, absolute Being, God, this alone and nothing more will be sufficient for me to feel that I must obey the decrees of his will even before he speaks or has expressly revealed his will to me. The obligation is already present within me solely through knowledge of this being; the mental conception of God supplies the obligating force. This obligating force is eternal; it is God himself in whom lies the intrinsic, immutable order of being.

191. But I do not need to know all this in order to be bound by a real obligation. The bond is perfect as soon as I feel the *exigency of the divine Being* by virtue of his very essence which is revealed to me (negatively) in the *mental conception* of his being. As I have said, it is possible that the supreme Being has not yet spoken, and that I have not yet reflected on his will; perhaps I am a simple human being who left to himself is unable to reflect on such great things. Nevertheless I am still bound by moral necessity, and if I resist, I am culpable.[117] This necessity does not bind through 'a command of a superior' but through 'the exigency I find and feel in the concept of a being (the supreme Being).' If this necessity were not a real, complete and very strict obligation, I would have no real, complete obligation to obey the command either of a superior or of God. But this is absurd. In this case not even the word 'God' could impose on me a more real, complete, rigorous obligation. If therefore what God commands and wills induces a real and complete obligation, we must accept that the 'exigency of the supreme Being which I feel in its very conception' is an equally real and complete obligation.

192. Hence, the *first form* of natural law and natural obligation is 'the exigency of the beings' conceived by us. This form is different from the form of a superior or of the decree of a Legislator; these forms belong to derived laws. In a word, the ULTIMATE REASON for our willingness to obey God as superior or execute the decree of God as Legislator is contained IN THE MENTAL CONCEPTION OF THE SUPREME BEING. The conception tells me that this being is essentially Superior and Legislator, and

[117] I offer these thoughts to P. Dmowski, who develops a contrary opinion in his Ethics.

hence MUST be obeyed. Thus the CONCEPT of that being manifests the being's MORAL EXIGENCY, which is obligation.[118]

193. Divine Scripture continually takes us back to this formal, ultimate reason of moral obligation, and wonderfully confirms the system which, as a matter of fact, I have attempted to draw solely from the word of God in Scripture and tradition. This will be obvious to lovers of truth by the many references to Scripture and the Fathers with which I have confirmed its truth in many places. I will now confirm it further by other references.

II.

The practical acknowledgement of beings according to truth is confirmed on the authority of Scripture

194. The principle of the practical acknowledgement of the truth, that is, of the beings we conceive, is indicated on nearly every page of Scripture. The way of speaking by which every virtue is called *truth*, and every vice *lie*, clearly demonstrates that the principle of morality is posited in the union of our will with beings in the way prescribed by truth. *Sinners* are called *liars*;[119] to have committed a crime is to have 'acted a lie;'[120] 'to do

[118] To say that the first obligation properly speaking cannot be called *law* is to reduce the matter to a question of words.

[119] Ps 115: 11 [Douai].

[120] 'From prophet to priest everyone deals falsely' (Jer 8: 10). And the inspired writer explains why what they do is a lie: they did not want *to acknowledge* their error; they considered themselves wise, knowing how to choose what was best, while in fact they did their worst because they opposed God's law. 'How can you say, "We are WISE, and the Law of the Lord is with us"? But, behold, the false pen of the scribes has made it into a LIE. The wise men shall be put to shame, they shall be dismayed and taken; lo, they have rejected the word of the Lord, and WHAT WISDOM IS IN THEM?' [Jer 8: 8–9]. — Also: 'Why do you love vanity and seek after LYING' (Ps 4: 3 [2 (Douai)]. In Hosea (7: 1 [Douai]): 'For they have committed FALSEHOOD.' In Isaiah: 'LYING sons' (30: 9), 'offspring of DECEIT'(57: 4). And speaking of the devil, Christ says: 'for he is a LIAR and the father of lies' (Jn 8: 44).

what is true' means to practise virtue.[121] In the sacred books 'the path of falsehood' frequently means the behaviour of a wicked person, 'the path of truth' the behaviour of a righteous person.[122]

195. This same admirable wisdom is also present in all those places where the word 'to know' indicates all other human actions, that is, actions virtually contained in knowledge. The knowledge in question is formed with the will's assent and is called practical, that is, OPERATIVE knowledge. According to this meaning, a person is blamed for 'not having known', or is praised for 'having known'; sinners are 'proud people who do not understand',[123] and are reproached for making themselves 'like the horse and the mule'.[124] The statement, 'They have not known the way of peace', means they have not followed the way of peace.[125] 'Not to know God' is the same as not to love or honour him.[126]

121 Jn 3: [21].

122 In Jeremiah (23: 14) we find: '. . . walk in lies'; in St. Peter (2nd letter, 2: 2) the author speaks of 'the way of truth'.

123 'The dull man CANNOT KNOW, the stupid CANNOT UNDERSTAND this' (Ps 91 [92: 6]). In psalm 35: [4 (Douai)] the words describing the unjust tell us that he speaks to himself in his heart to persuade himself that God does not see: 'The WORDS of his mouth are iniquity and guile: he would NOT UNDERSTAND that he might do well' (he did not want to acknowledge truth practically — if he had, he would have done good, but this he did not want). In psalm 94: [11 (Douai)] God swears that he will not let sinners enter into his rest because they did not *know his ways*.

124 Ps 31 [32: 9]. Similarly, in Isaiah 1: [3], the prophet reproaches Israel for 'not having known' its Lord, although the ox knows its owner, and the ass recognises his master's crib. Such ways of speaking are frequent in Scripture (cf. Jer 8); they clearly indicate the *practical knowledge* which is the true *efficient cause* of action. Hence there is never practical knowledge without consequent action, which explains why one is taken for the other, the cause for the effect.

125 Ps 13: [3 (Douai)]: 'Destruction and unhappiness in their ways; and THE WAY OF PEACE THEY HAVE NOT KNOWN: there is no fear of God before their eyes. The phrase, 'there is no fear of God before their eyes,' shows how an evil will turns the intellect's attention elsewhere to prevent the intellect's fixing itself in truth and loving it.

126 Cf. ftns. 123, 124. In Jeremiah 4 the prophet asks why the people flee the battle. The Lord replies: 'Because, my foolish people *have not known me*. They are *senseless* and *foolish* children. They are wise in doing evil, but do not know how to do good.' These last words recall those of St. Paul: 'Be prudent in doing good, and simple in evil', words which show how the knowledge of

196. The faculty of (speculative) *knowledge* is necessary; the faculty of (practical) *acknowledgement* is subject to our freedom. This distinction between these two faculties is clearly seen in the following well-known passage from Isaiah: 'Go, and say to this people: "Hear and hear, but do not understand; see and see, but do not perceive." Make the heart of this people fat, and their ears heavy, and shut their eyes; lest they see with their eyes, and hear with their ears, and understand with their hearts, and turn and be healed.'[127] The phrases, 'see with their eyes, hear with their ears and know with their hearts', express very aptly the willed act of *acknowledgement* (frequently mentioned in Scripture) as if those who know something without willing it do not see with their eyes or hear with their ears or know with their hearts. The eyes, ears and heart are personal and proper to the *human person* only in so far as they are controlled by the will; basically they belong to human nature, not to human beings themselves. Thus Joshua told the Hebrews that they would *know with all their mind* the fulfilment of the divine promises.[128]

197. In Scripture *acknowledgement* of one's faults and their expression by external confession always presuppose the willed act of the intellect we are discussing.[129] We are told, for example, that a wicked person does not obey the *truth*, that he is not satisfied with the truth, that he withdraws from it, and resists it.

good and of evil are for the most part freely chosen, because the will determines the intellect to apply itself to one thing rather than another.

127 Is 6: [9–10]. Similar expressions are found in common speech, as well as in Scripture: 'See and know' (1 Kg 24; 12 [Douai]; 'Hear and know' (Is 33: 13 [Douai]); 'Know and understand' (Jer 26: 15 [Douai]), etc. These expressions show the difference between the two faculties.

128 23: [14 (Douai)]: 'You shall know with all your mind'; similarly, Ps 138: [14 (Douai)]: 'I will praise you, for you are fearfully magnified: wonderful are your works and MY SOUL KNOWS RIGHT WELL.' Whenever God gives evidence of himself, Scripture says he makes himself known; holy men say they have known him whenever they internally admire his great work. For example, in the following passages: Ex 18: [11 (Douai)], Jethro says: 'Now I *know* that the Lord is great above all gods'; Ps 9: [17 (Douai)]: 'The Lord shall be *known* when he executes judgments'; Ps 118: [75 (Douai)]: 'I *know*, O Lord, that the judgments are equity,' and in other similar ways, as can be seen in Ps 134: [5 (Douai)] and many other places.

129 Ps 50 [51: 3]: 'I KNOW MY TRANSGRESSIONS. Cf. similar expressions in Ps 59: [3] and Jer 14: [20], etc.

The just person, on the other hand, rejoices in the *truth*.[130] Truth is characteristic of justice and holiness: 'the justice of truth', 'the holiness of truth.' The same is said about faith, which is called 'faith of the truth'.[131]

Knowledge of an action is taken for the *action* itself, that is, the cause for the effect. This gives rise to expressions like 'the ox knows its owner', 'the sun knows its setting'.[132]

Scripture's way of speaking often shows that the false, culpable judgment of the intellect is caused by the will directing the judgment's attention away from what it dislikes to what it likes — Isaiah says: 'They do not know neither do they understand; they are given over to darkness because their eyes have not seen nor did they *understand with their heart*. They do not consider in their mind; they do not know or hear.'[133] In the same way, the intellect's partiality for what it is thinking of is very well expressed by the scriptural phrase, 'to know the person of a human being' in judging, or 'to know someone's face'.[134]

When Christ says that 'he will not know those who have not known him', 'he is not known by the world', 'his sheep know him', etc., he expresses not only the supernatural light given to his followers but the willed attention to his divine prerogatives which would have produced love and esteem for the prerogatives, and encountered as it were the grace that came towards them.[135]

God says that 'among all the peoples, he knew only Israel'.[136] This expression, used of God, refers to what takes place in

[130] Gal 5: [7]: 'obeying the truth'; Rom 2: [8]: 'who do not obey the truth'; Tit 1: [14]: 'of men who reject the truth'; 2 Tim 3: [8]: 'oppose the truth': 1 Cor 13: [6 (Douai)]: 'rejoice with the truth'.

[131] Cf. Eph 4: [24 (Douai)]: 'In justice and holiness of truth'; 2 Thess 2: [13]: ' by belief in the truth'. A phrase similar to these is found in John: 'consecrated in truth' (17: [19]).

[132] Is 1: [3], Jer 8: [7], Ps 103 [104: 19].

[133] Is 44: [18–19].

[134] Prov 24: [23 (Douai)]: 'It is not good to have respect to persons in judgment'; 28: [21 (Douai)]: 'He that has respect to a person in judgment does not well.'

[135] Jn 1: 10; 10: 14 etc.

[136] Amos 3: [2]: 'You only have I *known* of all the families of the earth.' Also: 'I *know* how many are your transgressions' (5: [12]).

[197]

human beings: the thing which human beings know, value and love the most is that to which they give most of their intellectual attention.

198. We see therefore that the word 'know' in sacred Scripture, and indeed generally in languages (and coming apparently from a very ancient tradition), has two distinct meanings corresponding to the two ways of knowing proper to human beings. One of these ways is direct apprehension, that is, theoretical knowledge; the other is free judgment of the thing apprehended, that is, practical knowledge. For example, in one place we read: 'Elijah came and they *did not know him* but they did to him all they wished.'[137] If we did not distinguish the two ways of knowing, it would seem a contradiction to inflict upon Elijah all the evil they wanted, but without knowing him. But the sentence means: 'They did not acknowledge him for the human being he was, worthy of love and esteem.' This way of speaking passed into common usage and resulted in gratitude being called *recognition* and *acknowledgement*, and ingratitude *lack of acknowledgement*.

199. In Scripture, 'not knowing' is the cause of punishment and reward. In Jeremiah, for example: 'I will bring evils upon this people, the FRUIT OF ITS THOUGHTS, because they did not hear my words and have rejected my law.'[138] And as a willed act of knowledge gives rise to all our morality in this life, Scripture, always faithful to itself, teaches that in the other life an act of knowledge will form the happiness of every human being: 'This is eternal life, that they KNOW you, the one true God, and him whom you have sent, Jesus Christ.'[139]

200. Finally Scripture wonderfully expresses the moral dependence of human affection and external action on truth. We hear the characteristic of an upright, effective love: 'Whom I love IN TRUTH;'[140] and of an upright action: 'Let us love not in word or speech but by act and TRUTH.'[141]

201. In the sacred books, therefore, the natural, necessary

[137] Mt 17: [12].
[138] Jer 6: [19].
[139] Jn 17: [3].
[140] 3 Jn 5: 1.
[141] 1 Jn 3: 18.

connection between our practical judgments and affections, and between our affections and external actions, is clearly expressed. By means of this connection our affection and actions are subject to the same self-justified law presented to our intellect, that is, the law of truth. Similarly, the first law is clearly that which commands us to 'acknowledge beings according to their exigency' or in equivalent words, 'to acknowledge truth practically'. From this first obligation the command of every superior receives its authority and obligating force.

III.

The notion of religion

202. A direct light, therefore, given to the human mind by its Author, reveals how majestic and awesome this Author is, and how, as Author of the light and of all things, he is worthy of all love, honour and obedience. God, as though keeping himself hidden from us, gives us this natural light, a divine ray and something entirely his, which leads us to him. Through it we know beings at their own level, and evaluate them correctly; when the object of our evaluation is the supreme Being, the evaluation exceeds every limit.

203. We immediately sense our duties to him; this is the principle of religion. Among these duties is that of listening to his sublime voice when he speaks. This is the faith we owe to revelation. And if he deigns to give us commandments, we have the further duty of keeping them, that is, of obeying the command and law of the supreme Superior and Legislator. These communications from God (whether through external revelation or through internal grace) and our corresponding duties enlarge and complement religion.

204. Such is the notion of religion. We will now examine briefly the relationship between *morality*, whose principle is the acknowledgement of truth in general, and *religion*, whose principle is the acknowledgement of the supreme Being.

IV.

Examination of the principal opinions about the relationship between morality and religion

205. There are four principal opinions about the relationship between *morality* and *religion*:

1. Morality and religion are entirely separate.
2. Religion is related to morality as a part is related to the whole.
3. Religion is not a part of morality; morality is a part of religion.
4. Finally, religion and morality are thought to be the same. This opinion is understood in different ways.

206. It is difficult to save the first opinion from the accusation of impiety that has always been attached to it. Common sense affirms that a religion without morality can no longer be real or adequate, while morality without religion is simply very imperfect and completely dead.

207. The second and third opinions contain a general truth. If morality is defined as 'the complex of duties and counsels which perfect human personship', religion clearly plays a role because it includes duties and moral counsels related to God.

Equally morality is part of religion. If religion is defined as 'the contact and affectionate union of human beings with God, and the means for maintaining this contact and union', then contact such as this, with the supremely holy Being, can take place only on condition that human beings observe, and intend to observe the whole moral law. Clearly the contact itself is essentially moral, and realised in the fullness of morality.

208. Religion and morality, therefore, when understood in their fullest natural extension without the division many would place between them are the same thing considered under two different aspects. Considered *ideally* and abstractly, that is, as duty, this single thing is called morality; considered *really*, that is, as contact with the most holy Being, with holiness itself, it is called religion. If we consider matters abstractly and theoretically, religion presents itself as part of morality; if we consider matters from a practical point of view — in which we see things

as they actually exist — morality presents itself as religion. Thus they differ conceptually, but not in reality.

209. We can now see the true sense of the fourth opinion. If nothing moral is excluded from religion, and nothing religious from morality, the two can easily be the same thing. But this is impossible if one is sacrificed to the other by calling 'religion' morality without religion, and 'morality' religion without morality. These two errors are still maintained today; the first in particular is supported by rationalist philosophers, who claim that we have no direct duties towards God; all our duties to the supreme Being are indirect, that is, reduced to duties to human beings.

210. Although morality and religion, considered in their totality and perfection, are the same reality, they are certainly different considered from the point of view of their varying development in the human spirit at different periods. The principle of *morality* is an abstract, ideal rule (the idea of being), while the principle of *religion* is a subsistent being (the conception or perception of the divinity). Because they begin from different points, they follow a different path. Only when they are at the end of their journey, and both are considered perfect, will they truly become perfectly identical. As long as they are on the way, as it were, to their goal, they are considered, and really are two things which, however, harmonise, perform mutually useful service and often mingle like currents in a river.

V.

The religious principle renders knowledge of moral duties easy for human beings

211. We will consider only a few of the great services that the religious principle renders morality still on its way to perfection. Let us see first of all how much the concept of a supreme Being and legislator helps the mind to develop moral knowledge in the most sure and enlightened way.

Human beings have difficulty in applying the principle of

morality to particular cases and deducing specific duties. The difficulty increases as the importance of the object to which the principle is applied decreases. Because the application of the moral law is made through a judgment about the excellence of objects, greater grades of excellence in an object make their acknowledgement easier. Equally, their disavowal, even when wilful, is more difficult. Because the error in question is greater and more obvious in these circumstances, we would have to do further violence to ourselves in order to make a false judgment. But once we have established the principle that the certainty and ease of application of the law depend on the greatness of the objects to which the principle is applied, it follows that our judgment, in the case of an object endowed with infinite dignity, will be very clear and unassailable

212. God is such an object. For this reason there is no human being so ignorant or people so primitive whose minds are not enlightened by the resplendent duty of honouring their supreme Maker. For the same reason some moralists posit the first law in God's will. According to them, our judgment about the respect due to the divine will contains the clearest possible evidence; there could be no clearer principle. But they do not reflect that the problem lies at the level of scientific knowledge. Our problem is not whether another principle is necessary, but simply whether there is an anterior principle in the order of ideas. The moralists of whom we are speaking have erred by not reflecting on this aspect of the question.

213. But when we have known the supreme Being, applied the law to the supreme legislator and deduced our duty of conforming our will to his, we have discovered a very sure, easy means of knowing all other moral duties, which can be reduced to positive cognition of the supreme will. Consequently, the way of knowing what God wills is beyond dispute for all who recognise a positive revelation made by the supreme Being to humankind and to a Church with infallible magisterium. Such people are relieved from the heavy and sometimes unbearable burden of endless, uncertain, fallacious reasonings in which passions always propose some compromise with truth. In Christianity therefore a single moral judgment acknowledging the supreme Being and his word sometimes exempts us from the necessity of other judgments, or of applying the principle of

morality to their actions. The easiest, most secure, clearest and universal way of applying the first law is acknowledgement of the divine legislator.

VI.

Religious sanction — its necessity

214. Rousseau said: 'Philosophers, your precepts are fine, but show me their sanction.'

It is a well known fact that morality does not find a sufficient sanction in nature, and that only the rewards and punishments of the future life can constitute such a sanction.[142] We have already noted that the only way to refute Carneades' sophistry (by which he tried to show that a human being would have to be stupid in order to be just) is recourse to the punishments and rewards of the future life.[143] This would in fact be sufficient to demonstrate the immense importance of religion for human morality. Hence religious belief was correctly considered the sole condition capable of making morality universally real for humanity and the only sufficient guarantee of mutual rights.[144]

[142] The word 'sanction', derived from [the Latin] '*sanctum, sanctitas*' [that which is holy, holiness] would seem to contain an ancient way of indicating a belief that the 'sanction' of laws and rights properly speaking appertains to religion itself.

[143] Lactantius writes: 'Those who reject the mystery of humanity and relate everything to this temporal life, cannot know how powerful justice is. They admit in their discussions that virtue is full of misery and trouble, but say it must be desired for its own sake, since they do not see any eternal rewards for it. Because everything is related to this present life, they reduce virtue to STUPIDITY. Virtue labours pointlessly and vainly in this life' (*D. Institutionum*, 5: 8).

[144] Some consider sanction as a constitutive element of right and refuse to recognise any right which lacks a corresponding sanction. I consider this opinion erroneous. However, we should note the strange, obvious incongruence of some writers who, after placing sanction among the constitutive elements of right, exclude all religion from the teaching on right. To be coherent they should have done the opposite. If their only sufficient sanction for rights lies in the punishments and rewards of the other life, it is clear that

VII.

The moral activity of the human race is rooted in the religious principle

215. However religion does more than that. An earthly sanction, sufficient to restrain us in all possible cases from doing evil, would satisfy the law of natural justice, which commands us to order our actions so that they do not oppose the exigency of things. But what kind of stimulus would we need for good actions? What law would have sufficient authority to prescribe the mode of action and make us act?

216. It is true that nature has sympathetic affections gently inclining us to love and do good to our neighbour. Philosophers did not delay in firmly attaching their shaky morality to them, but the effort was soon seen to fail. Good sense saw that

in their very way of thinking religious sanction has become a constitutive of human rights. Consequently no right can exist without religion.

In Italy, Romagnosi included sanction in the definition of right and, not satisfied with this, made the *authority* of natural right itself consist in sanction. He says: 'We have already seen that the predominant, essential characteristic of any law consists in establishing the necessity for doing or omitting something. Whenever a natural law is affirmed for human beings, a higher order of causes and forces is considered to exist in nature. Through these causes and forces we are bound to do or omit certain free acts as *indispensable* means towards obtaining something better and avoiding something worse (§1 and 2). The strength of law consists in the power by which it establishes this necessity. The authority of the natural law therefore consists in this higher force which is able to produce something good or evil as part of certain human acts in such a way that human power, *wishing* to obtain good and avoid evil, is constrained to obey this authority of nature' (*Assunto Primo etc.*, §4). — Clearly Romagnosi did not have a correct idea of right and law. He turns to *physical necessity* to explain the *obligation*, and posits the *authority* of natural law in this necessity. He was totally unaware therefore of the nature of *moral necessity*, the real *authority* of law, by which law binds souls, not bodies, with a bond whose nature differs from that of physical force. Physical force, no matter how great we conceive it, could never bind in this way, nor release the intelligent soul it might have already bound.

Romagnosi's mind saw only *real* things. He vainly tried to rise to the world of *ideas* but always fell back on physical reality. We must not attribute this to mental debility but to the false school of the period in which he was educated. The sensism of Bonnet trapped him in material sensations from which his natural powers could not extricate him.

sympathetic affection and gentle inclinations did not contain the authority of law. Subject to illusions and eccentricities, and even to serious disorders, they also vary capriciously in different individuals, and sometimes lead us to offend rather than practise virtue. Affections, therefore, could not be considered the principle of the moral activity necessary for individuals, for society and for the human race. Moreover, even if we found affections on the same level and with the same nature in everyone, and free from the restrictions we have mentioned, we would still have to take account of their uncertain, tenuous power. Their weakness would be a matter for concern even if we did not abandon ourselves to their blind action, but subjected their impulses to the dictates of natural reason (which, without religion, is itself a limited, fallacious norm). Such affections could not resist our self-love for long, nor produce the great moral activity which comes from religion alone. Their sole effect would consist in some miserable, perhaps sterile, activity.

217. On the other hand, the sublime concept of God communicated to the human race by the Gospel has all the necessary characteristics to be, here on earth, the principle of an unlimited moral activity, especially when the principle is enlightened by grace. I shall make only a few observations to demonstrate this.

First of all, our moral judgment about God, granted we know him, must obviously respect him as an object of the greatest reverence and adoration. He is present to our mind as the absolute Being and therefore the source of being. The universe, which is nothing compared with him, receives its existence from him at every moment. We ourselves, tiny particles of the universe, would be doubly nothing if he did not communicate to us all that we are. Just as we receive being from him, so only from him can we expect the increase of our existence, that is, every perfection. And if he is our principle, he is also our end, the ocean and inexhaustible fount of good, of all the good that can be an object of our desire.

218. We have seen that the cause of all our movement is the desire for, and esteem of good. If our judgment about the supreme Being becomes *practical*, as religion requires it to be, the supreme Being must obviously become for us the end and

reason of all our actions. The moral law, considered in its general concept but not yet applied to subsistent beings, does not command us to perform actions; it simply imposes the *manner* of their performance. But when we begin to apply the law to God, it reveals him as the source of *positive* obligations; it no longer commands or counsels only the manner of our actions but the actions themselves.

219. The supreme Being, therefore, both legislator and rewarder of those who do good, is the source of the most exquisite moral actions. When the law is applied to him, it almost seems to change nature, assuming a tone equally authoritative but more demanding. It does not say: 'I leave you free to do, or not to do the actions; but when you do them, you must do them in conformity with the truth.' It says: 'Act with all your powers to attain the supreme Good.'

Before we knew the supreme Good, it would have been difficult to understand how our actions could be made obligatory relative to both their manner and their being. As I have observed, there would seem to be no way of reconciling the principle of happiness with that of virtue, although we cannot renounce either one or the other. However, once the supreme Good is known, the law can command the *actions themselves*, not simply their *manner* of being, because the precept of directing our actions to the supreme Good remains perfectly in accord with our natural inclination to happiness.

220. We cannot say however that a similar precept arises from the inclination to happiness. In fact the precept arises uniquely from the force of what is true. If we note the process by which the precept reveals itself, we see how it draws all its obligating force from pure justice. As soon as we have known God directly, we must make the practical judgment that he is our supreme Good; the bare force of truth and pure justice oblige us to this judgment. Because he is our supreme Good, we must judge him to be so.

221. The discovery, in this judgment, of our supreme advantage is a consequence of the judgment, and does not constitute the explanation of or necessity for the judgment, which is right because it is true, not because it is useful. On the other hand, the infinite utility attached to the obligation simply renders its realization possible. Only religion, therefore, the holy and

blessed concept of God, offered by Christianity, constitutes the sufficient *principle* of human *moral activity*.

222. For this reason the gospel formula, proclaimed as the formula which contains the first and supreme commandment, was pronounced by Christ in a positive, not a negative form. He commands actions to be done, not how they are done. Indeed he commands the greatest activity possible, drawing all human powers into movement. He says: 'You shall love the Lord your God with all your heart, and with all your soul, and with all your mind. — You shall love your neighbour as yourself.'[145]

It is now time to discuss the essence of right.

[145] Mt 22: [37, 39]. Here we must note that the command is to love God with all our *mind*, that is, with the act of willed *acknowledgement* of his supreme perfection and goodness. 'With all our *heart*' expresses our spiritual *affections*. 'With all our soul' means with our whole animal life at every moment of life. St. Mark [12: 30] and St. Matthew [St. Luke 10: 27] add 'with all your strength' to recall what has been said in the preceding phrases and to indicate that every action of our life must be sacred to the supreme Being, and carried out with all the energy of our spirit. All this seems to recall the expression in Deuteronomy 4: [6: 4] 'with all your might'. — Pagan philosophers, when they wanted to demonstrate the *positive* duty of benevolence which we have to others, had recourse to God as the common father of all (cf. Cicer. *De Offic.*, bk. 3, c. 6).

These things arise because we are naturally inclined to love our fellows, which is the foundation of right.

Cicero. *De Leg.*, 1: 15.

THE ESSENCE OF RIGHT

THE NATURE OF RIGHT:
ITS RELATIONSHIP WITH DUTY

223. The *principle* of Right is the first object of research in jural philosophy. This principle is simply the most general idea of right. Any *principle*, in fact, is only an *idea* considered in its aptitude for being applied.[146]

The *idea*, or concept, contains the *essence* of some thing:[147] the idea or concept of right contains and makes known the nature and essence of right. This essence, when known and capable of being seen, can be recognised in those actions which share in it. In other words, rights can be *derived from* their *principle*.

The *concept* of any thing is also expressed in the thing's definition. Our first aim, therefore, is to define right; we shall then subject the definition to analysis; and finally we shall compare *right* with *duty* and establish the relationship between them.

CHAPTER 1
The definition of right

224. Common sense maintains and always has maintained that *right* is different from *force*. Often it goes so far as to see opposition between *force* and *right*.

Force is sometimes employed to *defend* right and sometimes to *violate* it.

[146] *OT*, 570–573.

[147] *OT*, 646.

When brute force is used to oppress human beings who possess right *per se*, other people show an extraordinary interest in the matter. From that moment on, right appears to shine with unusual splendour. It triumphs, in fact, because it renders itself immune to violent action. It acts as an immortal entity, out of reach of all material power which tries in vain to touch it. All the efforts made by material force are excluded from the high, spiritual sphere where right has its home. In a word, *right*, no less than *duty*, is an ideal, moral entity whose source has to be found where we find the source of duty, that is, where in fact we find will and law.

Will is the power through which, by acknowledging the objects which present themselves to our understanding, we either adhere to them and thus fulfil our duty, or disavow them. Two terms have to be distinguished in the volitive power: the principle of action, which is the will or *subject* (human being) itself, and the term of action, that is, the *objects* set before the subject.

225. As we have seen in discussing the *Moral System*, law begins to shine in us from objects when their exigency manifests itself to our intelligence. Law is itself the exigency; law is duty intimated to us; and the science of duty is called *morals*.

Pleasure comes from the *subject*, of which it is a modification; and the science of pleasure is what we have called *eudaimonology*. *Pleasure* taken in its broadest sense as eudaimonological good constitutes *right* when it is protected by law emanating from the object.

226. To find the distinct, accurate definition of right, and all the elements which compose it, we have to meditate and analyse the act of will that contains in itself the source of right and the source of duty. Let us do this as carefully as we can.

227. When we recollect ourselves in order to contemplate an object, we say willingly, without any hesitation or withdrawal on the part of the will: 'This object is beautiful, good, worthy and precious.' And our act is *just* if the object is the same when we affirm it as when we apprehend it.

In this case, our soul, undisturbed by bitterness arising from a desire for something which would hinder its full assent to the object, sees the object and fixes its attention entirely upon its beauty, goodness, worth and excellence (which every object possesses in some way). As a result, the soul experiences delight and enjoyment in the object. This delight rises within the soul from an intimate, hidden law which links the *intellective soul* to *being*, to the whole of being and to every entity. We call this *love* 'appreciative' because it is an affection carried over from the act of esteem with which we judge some thing favourably and willingly.[148]

228. Nevertheless, the act of simple, willed acknowledgment has a nature distinct from such enjoyment, which follows and springs from this act as heat does from light. Knowing is the proper act of the intellect. Its effect in the soul, the subject of the intellective potency, is joy or delight on account of the known object. The subject, in so far as it is susceptible of such feelings, is called *spirit*, *heart*, and so on.

229. We have to note, however, that the subject or the soul does not experience a pleasurable feeling only from its union with acknowledged objects; it draws pleasure also from the use of any of its powers which achieves the end for which it exists. The presence of an object is sufficient, therefore, for the soul to experience enjoyment, but an intellective subject is necessary if

[148] I have no intention of abandoning the ancient distinction between *love* and *joy*. For me, *love* is the tendency to good, and *joy* is contentment in the possession of what is good. My sole comment is that human beings must first acknowledge what is good as good before they can tend towards possession of it. Simply by acknowledging it as such, they rejoice in it from afar. Delight in *love* is one thing, therefore; delight in *joy* properly so-called is another. The first kind of delight comes from simple contemplation of what is good; the second from its complete, real possession. The intellective soul unites itself to its objects either through the *species* which informs the soul's knowledge if the real object is not *per se* intelligible, or through real, immediate union if it is *per se* intelligible. — The ancients attributed *love* even to inanimate things. This would be only a metaphorical way of expressing things in our manner of speaking. For the ancients, however, it had real meaning because of their definition of love. They called love 'unitive force', a definition inherent to the etymology of the word. At the very beginning of philosophy, 'love' was properly used of physical love, and metaphorically of moral love. This is a constant, regulatory law in the use of words which were first invented to express physical things such as the attraction of bodies. Their use was then extended metaphorically to embrace spiritual things, for example, the attraction and union of spirits. Finally, the first meaning was forgotten; words were reserved to signify spiritual things alone, for which they became proper. Unless I am mistaken, this is the history of the meanings of the words *to love*, *love*, etc., and of the word *sin*. Cf. vol. 4, *Opere morali*, pp. 193–196.

intellectual enjoyment is to be present, that is, enjoyment springing from the light and good present in things which have been understood.

All *enjoyment* begins and ends, therefore, within the subject; enjoyment is so simple that it has no terms, but perfect unicity. All *knowledge*, on the other hand, bears the subject into an object outside the subject itself. Consequently, it has two terms, the knower and that which is known.

230. This proves that the simple act of acknowledgement does not depend on the delight that succeeds it, but on the energy proper to a will freely obeying the exigency manifested by objects which, in this way, impose law upon the will. But while the intelligent subject is thus morally necessitated to humble itself and as it were depend upon objects which make themselves known and which it cannot change, it benefits from its subjection and spontaneous passivity. It achieves its own perfection by adhering to beings themselves through the act of knowledge, through reception of the truth, and through carrying out the law. But there is no physical coercion in all this; hence the presence of moral freedom.

231. *Moral freedom* arises from the opposition between object and subject. The latter, as subject, without reference to the law that it receives from the object, is guided by instinct; the former on the contrary imposes a law on the subject by prescribing a way of action which conforms to what is true, but without any reference to instinct as instinct. Both *instinct* and *law*, each in its own way, determine human actions, but the determination brought about by instinct often finds itself in opposition to the determination imposed by the law. One determination collides with the other and remains suspended, as it were. At this point, the human being is not necessitated by either determination. He can choose, making use of one or other of the two determining principles. And this is freedom.

232. Because the law is inflexible, we always feel morally obliged by it, but without physical constraint. Nevertheless, the obligation itself, felt continually through the unceasing stimulation provided by its relentless voice, provokes and strengthens us to act rightly. The germ of moral force within us is first *our feeling* of duty and then our *consciousness* of it.

233. This force or moral energy belongs to each one of us. It

is we ourselves who, as intelligent subjects, act contrary to ourselves as feeling subjects. The subject has become 'person'; 'person' stands opposed to the merely instinctive subject. And we ourselves are that person.[149] We are the authors, therefore, of what we do, and of the praise or blame, the merit or demerit, of our actions. We have real governance over what we do, and must take account of this governance as an element of right.

234. Indeed, the concept of right supposes in the first place a person, the author of his own actions. If a body moves, the action adheres to the body, but the body cannot be called its author. Body is passive; it neither wants to act, nor knows how to act. It does not act; action is done in it. The laws of motion of body are fixed; they depend upon its nature, but this nature does not depend upon ITSELF. Its motion does not proceed from ITSELF because ITSELF does not exist. And in the last analysis, even the actions of brute animals are not proper to their subject. The instinct determining these actions does not depend upon the subject, but upon the nature of the subject which has been constituted by the author of the universe. In order that beings may be called authors of their own actions, it is necessary for THEMSELVES to do these actions. THEY THEMSELVES exist only if they know and they will — in a word, if they are *persons.*[150]

235. *Freedom* — this governance with which we posit and rule our actions — is however a *de facto*, but not yet a *de jure* seigniory. Although we possess freedom, by means of which we can determine our actions in favour of, or against the law, we act badly every time we make use of freedom to determine actions in opposition to the law, and we act well every time we make use of it to determine them according to the law. This is what we call moral good and evil. We have physical freedom, therefore, but not yet truly *moral* freedom, which is present only when

[149] The teaching on personship has been set out by me in *AMS*, bk 4, to which I refer the reader.

[150] This teaching is admitted by all. Nevertheless, no one, as far as I know, has realised how pregnant it is with ontological consequences. The proposition, 'There are no true causes other than intelligent causes', when considered carefully, is sufficient to rectify the common manner of thinking about external nature and of conceiving its powers.

freedom's actions are in accordance with the limits defined by the moral law.

236. *Moral freedom*, therefore, is that part of physical freedom which is not restricted by the moral law. This is not only *de facto* freedom but also freedom *de jure*. And it is here, in moral freedom, that *right*, whose notion we were seeking, begins to appear. Absolutely and properly speaking, we cannot have a true right to do an action forbidden by the moral law (and by moral law we mean any law which morally obliges). The reason is clear: what is wrong cannot be right. But this is not sufficient. We have to add that the word *right* indicates something over and above what is simply *licit*. It indicates not simple freedom, but a certain *authority* or governance to act, which of its nature involves a relationship with other people. This relationship is formed by the moral law itself which simultaneously grants freedom of action to a person and prohibits others from interfering with that action.

237. Our definition of right may, therefore, be expressed in the way we noted in the Introduction. Right is a moral governance or authority to act, or: right is a faculty to do what we please, protected by the moral law which obliges others to respect that faculty.

CHAPTER 2

Analysis of the definition of right

238. This definition contains the general notion, which is found in all rights. But before reducing the definitions of special rights to the general definition, we have to analyse the latter and consider separately each of the elements which compose it. The notion of right, which we have expressed in our definition, consists of five elements:

1st. The existence of subjective activity;

2nd. The existence of *personal activity*, that is, activity exercised by the subject by means of rational will (freedom);

3rd. Exercise of this activity (an exercise which is *good*, not useless, for its author);

4th. *Lawful* exercise of the same activity ('lawful' means not opposed to the moral law);

5th. Finally some relationship with other rational beings on whom rests the duty of respecting our activity (the activity is exercised under the *protection* of the moral law).

Let us consider these elements separately.

Article 1.
The first element of right: the activity of a subject

239. The word *activity* has to be taken here in a very broad sense as, for instance, when we say that everything entering the feeling of a subject supposes some activity and actuality on the part of the subject which must at least leave itself open to the experience and co-operate with the modification it receives. Although the concept of *feeling* involves that of *passivity*, there is no doubt that the existence of passivity in the subject could not be conceived without some corresponding activity in the subject itself.[151] — We have to say this to avoid giving the impression that we exclude pleasurable, passive feelings experienced by the subject from the matter of right.

Note also that pleasurable feelings are usually the effect of the subject's actions, and that the very activity of the subject intervenes to preserve and defend them. Finally, we observe that the subject's *de facto* dominion of its actions is that which determines it to omit actions which could impede, remove or disturb pleasurable feelings. Consequently, the intellective subject's apparent inactivity contains some act of will.

Right, therefore, always has as its *basis* some faculty or activity of the human being.[152]

[151] Cf. *AMS*, 367–369.

[152] The reader should note that here we are setting out a kind of technical language which we intend to maintain faithfully throughout the whole of this work — provided we are not the victim of some involuntary distraction. The

Article 2.
The second element of right: personal activity

240. As we have said, the person is the supreme, active principle of an intelligent subject. Personal activity, therefore, supposes intelligence; it is the will in the subject which determines the subject as a result of the knowledge received from things. Of itself, a blind instinct cannot therefore constitute any right.

241. Physical action as found in material beings and in the blind, sensuous instinct of brute animals is not sufficient to establish the existence of a right. Intelligence must be present, together with will, the consequence of intelligence in the human being. Only will has the power to determine actions in accordance with intelligence and thus to give human beings the supreme prerogative of being and of calling themselves the *authors* and, therefore, masters of what they do.

242. The belief of previous ages that beasts were capable of rights was undoubtedly an error, which perhaps has not yet been totally abandoned. They are incapable of right because they are incapable of possessing *de facto dominion* of what they do, a capacity presupposed by the notion of *de jure right*. Roman laws, having established natural right common to beasts, opened the floodgates to errors which have unfortunately persisted for many centuries. The authors of these laws grasped the *first element* of right, that is, subjective action, but they had no clear, constant vision of the *second element*, that is, of personal action. They saw the isolated action which is only the material part of right; they were almost completely oblivious to the formal part [*App.*, no. 1]. When Roman jurisprudence flourished once more, some theorists attributed rights to beasts, and seriously undertook the examination of the legal procedures to be used if animals had to be punished! These theorists lacked a clear idea of what constituted right precisely because Roman laws did not provide it.

subject of right, therefore, will always be the person who possesses the right; *basis of right* will always refer to the *faculty* which forms the first element of right. Authors occasionally call this faculty the 'immediate object' of right, but we think it better to apply the word 'object' to the *good* we wish to obtain or use with the *faculty*.

243. The efforts made by some sophists to degrade human beings to the level of brute animals do not merit attention here. The thinkers were quite open about deducing the only legitimate conclusions of the sensist system and, as publicists, applied their humiliating theories to society and to the noble teaching of equality and social freedom which they degraded and debased to the core.

244. The systems of philosophers of antiquity on the transmigration of souls, or on the soul of the world and a divinity infused through all the branches of nature, did contain lengthy questions on the respect due to beasts. These theories, however, raise no objections to the teaching we have expounded because the problem of rights in beasts only arose after discussion about the existence of reason in beasts.[153]

The desire to diminish ferocity and cruelty in savage human beings was perhaps another reason why ancient sages invented systems in which beasts appeared as worthy of respect. Many laws were established by ancient legislators in favour of beasts in the hope that when people had ceased to ill-treat them, they would also be restrained from slaughtering one another. At the time of Hesiod, for example, it was seen and taught without equivocation that justice and law, right and duty, were proper to human beings alone.[154]

245. Finally, I have to note that the personal, free activity of which we are speaking and which is necessary as a constitutive element of right, does not always have to be in second act, as they say in the schools. It is sufficient for the action to belong *of its nature* to human dominion. Even if accidentally withdrawn from the free power of a human being, this activity still forms part of his *ownership* because it is such by natural law. The individual could take up once more the exercise of his power

[153] The discussion amongst philosophers of antiquity about what was due to beasts became another pretext used by Carneades for denying clear knowledge of justice to human beings. Cf. the *Republica Ciceroniana* discovered by his Eminence Cardinal Mai, bk. 3, §2. Further details may be found in Pufendorf, *De Jure Nat. et Gent.*, 4: 3.

[154] 'Law was given to humankind by Jove, the supreme; beasts, fishes, and birds that fly above eat one another because they lack that best of things, law, which extends no further than us' (*Oper. et Dier.*, vv. 276 ss.).

over the activity as soon as the accidental circumstances impeding or suspending it had changed.

We have to understand that 'if any cause whatsoever renders spontaneous an action which could be free in a human being, we cannot conclude that some other individual can dispose of this action without violating the right of the person concerned. In this case, the action posited still belongs by nature to the person doing it, who can always reasonably claim ownership to it.' The fact is that the personal nature of an action does not depend properly speaking upon its indifferent freedom, but on the personship of the principle from which it emanates.

However, we shall develop the notion of *ownership* later (as we have seen, it forms part, as a consequence of personship, of the concept of right). For the moment, we shall draw an important corollary from the two constitutive elements of right which we have so far explained.

Article 3.
Corollary of the two elements of right explained so far: right is accompanied by coercion

246. Knowing that right is a faculty, an activity, a governance (we can use the words indifferently), we are able to affirm clearly the corollary that the exercise of right includes force. The force with which right is exercised and put into act is the origin of *coercion*, acknowledged by all as something intimately connected with right itself.

The necessity of an intimate connection between right and force is seen even more clearly if we consider that we are dealing with *personal activity*, the highest of all activities even from a physical point of view because it rules *de facto* over all other activities which it employs as instruments and means for itself. This allows us to conclude that the coercion connected with right generally speaking is as great as the whole complex of governance within a person. We can, therefore, exercise our right with all the forces at our disposition, using them to repel all opposition and even to compensate for the good lost by injury inflicted upon us.

247. Nevertheless, the measure of coercion, which is very extensive when considered without relationship to its circumstances, is limited by the moral duties resulting from accidental circumstances, about which we shall speak in the appropriate place. For the moment, we have to deal with an important question: 'Does coercion have to form part of the definition of right?'

248. Some authors effectively put coercion in the definition. Their stance could be strengthened by the following argument: 'Right is a personal activity; but in the concept of activity we already find the concept of force and coercion; therefore the notion of right already contains in itself the use of force, that is, coercion.'

This reasoning contains a basis of truth, but it is not sufficiently strong. Its concepts, weakened by lack of clarity, are rather confused. Some distinctions have to be made if the argument is to rendered as clear as it should be.

249. There is no doubt that every activity and faculty contains force, but not universally in second act, as we said. It is always present, but only in first act, that is, in potency. But if right sometimes consists in a mere faculty or potential activity it can indeed be said that the concept expressed in its definition includes force in potency, but not necessarily force in act. We have to distinguish, therefore, between *primitive right*, which consists in a *potential faculty*, and the exercise of this primitive right which can appropriately be called *secondary right* and consists in an *actuated faculty*.

250. Right consisting in a mere faculty is injured every time the faculty itself is injured; right consisting in the act of the faculty is injured whenever the act is impeded. Both the right consisting in the faculty and that consisting in the act of the faculty can be defended with force in so far as either can be injured. But in every case the use of force requires some act. Consequently, the right to use force cannot consist in a faculty in a state of mere potency, but must be a right proper to an actuated faculty. Note, however, that the right to use force is not, properly speaking, a special class of rights consisting in an actuated faculty; it is an accident, as it were, manifested in the exercise of one's own right.

251. The question can, therefore, be answered as follows:

'Force is only coercive in a right if it is found in the *de facto* activity of the subject of right; but it does not adhere essentially to any right of the subject.' We can conclude that force sufficient to defend a right is not necessary to constitute that right, as some authors have unreasonably upheld. The consequence of such savage teaching is that authors sacrifice the rights of the weak,[155] which are no less sacred than the rights of the strong. It is the rights of the weak which deserve to be defended at least by the protestations and writings of wise people as they impress more deeply on all human hearts the conviction already implanted by nature: that is, rights remain inviolate although no defence is present to safeguard and protect them.

Article 4.
The third element: some good present in the action

252. An action without value or pleasing consequence for the person performing it could not be the object of a true right. Right must always be referred to some good, to something pleasing to human nature. This is so necessary that we can establish the principle: 'Mere caprice can never be the object of any right.' Things were, in fact, taken to such an extreme that ridiculous abstractions were used to establish stupid rights, useless to those who were supposed to possess them and harmful to others. It is time for such abstractions to give way to more complex thought. Crude yet strangely sophisticated right, by which publicists and even moralists often give their seal of approval to serious damage, has to stop.

When I speak of some good or of something pleasing, I consider this good from the eudaimonological point of view. In other words, I consider it in the *natural* relationship it can have with human satisfaction or even with happiness. Nevertheless, the good of which we are speaking could also be moral good which has amongst its results and consequences a natural order

[155] Some modern authors use this principle to despoil the Church of her rights. They say: 'The Church has no arms or defence forces, and therefore has no rights. These all belong to the State.'

related to our satisfaction and happiness. In this way, moral good, too, can be considered as eudaimonological good.

253. We need to add, however, that this good which intervenes to constitute a right must be inherent to the subject in such a way that the mere privation of the right would cause harm to the subject. If the case concerned some good not adhering to the subject, but entirely separate from him and obtainable only through the subject's action, this good would not be sufficient to constitute a right. The subject could, in fact, remain deprived of the good without suffering any pain concomitant on the privation. The good connected with the action, or comprised in the action, is that which gives worth to the action and as such is the end, the object of the right.

254. Allow me to note here that this element of right, in attracting the attention of some of the ancients, appears to have suggested to them the title 'right of nature'. They used this expression to indicate 'right founded in the natural instincts for conservation, procreation, etc.; right having as its object the needs and good things desired by nature, *quod natura omnia animalia docuit* (because it seems that need and instinct teach the animal to seek satisfaction from them).'

Others realised that this concept lacked the formal part of right found in reason alone. As a result they substituted human nature for nature in general. Human nature has animal instincts as the beasts have, but it also possesses superior instincts, needs and rational good, all of which rule over merely animal instinct. Cicero expresses this admirably: 'The nature of right is to be sought in the NATURE OF HUMAN BEINGS.[156]

Having arrived at this point, the human mind knew that *good* as the object of right had to be *human good*, not merely animal good. In other words, it had to be referred to a rational being, or person. The mind was now prepared to uncover another truth and find another meaning in the word *nature*, which it had assumed as a pointer to right. Instead of considering nature in the *subject*, the mind could consider it as *object*. This step was

[156] *De Leg*. 1: 5. — Grotius also used this accurate expression. For instance, he says: 'And whatever is obviously opposed to such a judgment is also against the right of NATURE, that is, HUMAN NATURE (*De jure* B *et* P. Prol. 9, 40, 41. Cf. also bk 1, c. 1, §11).

easy, as I said, because in human nature subject and object are not confused but joined. Nature as object indicates to the mind moral exigencies very different from the requirements of instincts. Consequently, 'live according to nature', the ancient precept which passed from the Socratic school to the almost exclusive use of the Stoics, received two quite different interpretations. If the word 'nature' is taken as *subject*, it means 'live according to the instincts and stimuli of our nature'; taken as object, it means 'live according to the exigencies and indications of the natures of things'. These two meanings were often mixed and confused by the greatest sages of antiquity, although the second meaning, the superior meaning, was not entirely lacking. Cicero, for instance, argues that we should love other human beings as ourselves because our *nature* is equal. Here *nature has* an objective sense, and philosophy already begins to reach out to the true moral principle of the practical acknowledgement of nature or beings.[157]

255. Returning to the point we were making, we may conclude: the third element of right is that 'the activity owned by the subject should have some eudaimonological value.'

Article 5.
The fourth element of right: the lawfulness of the action

256. In the fourth place, right can only be a faculty to do what is intrinsically upright and lawful. We have already explained why this is so: it is clear that there is no right to do things which are morally evil. It follows that if an action were *per se* upright but degraded through a wrong intention on the part of the one who does it, or through his ordering it towards some perverse

[157] 'If this is the case with NATURE, so too in their JUDGMENT' (this is the judgment, the acknowledgement) 'right would be cultivated by all. As the poet says: humans think that nothing human is alien to themselves. — This shows that an almost incredible act is done in the eyes of some people when one wise man bestows such extensive benevolence upon another endowed with equal virtue. Nevertheless, this act is necessary if he is TO LOVE ANOTHER NO LESS THAN HIMSELF. How does he differ, all things being equal?' The whole of this beautiful passage may be found in *De Legib.*, 1:12.

end, or for any other reason, the person concerned goes beyond the limits of his right.

257. Nevertheless, if one person attempts to despoil another of his faculty for carrying out *per se* upright actions (to which he has a true right), he would do him an injury. This would not be the case if an attempt were made to impede the abuse of the right, provided that the person wishing to stop the abuse had a right to do so[158] — in other words, provided there were no obligatory law forbidding him to make the attempt.

258. However, *lawfulness* in an action, which is necessary if the action is to be subject to right, is defined in different ways by various authors. The diversity depends upon the aim they had in view when establishing the constitutive elements of right, and therefore according to the legislation to which they refer this lawfulness.

In Germany, natural right is considered solely as a basis for the external, positive legislation of the State. In this case, *lawfulness*, which is required in order that a right may be possible, is the result of the external laws of the State, or at most, the result of immunity from natural coercion. In other words, my right to carry out these actions is established on the basis that other people are unable to impede my actions with the use of force.

Counsellor Zeiller explained the matter as follows in his natural-private Right:

> Right is not a moral faculty in the strictest sense so that we have a right only to what is morally good and compatible with virtue, nor is right to be numbered amongst internally lawful things. I say this because it cannot be denied that we

[158] St. Thomas puts the matter very well: 'Human nature is changeable; consequently, what is natural to human beings is sometimes less than it should be. For instance, natural equity requires that what has been deposited should be repaid to the person who deposits it. If nature were always what it should be, this would always have to be done. Sometimes, however, the human will is turned to evil, and in this case it occasionally happens that the deposit need not be returned, *ne homo perversam voluntatem habens MALE EO UTATUR ut puta si furiosus vel hostis reipublicae arma deposita reposcat* [in order to prevent a person with bad will FROM USING IT BADLY. For example, an aggressive person or an enemy of the State might ask for the return of the weapons he has handed in]' (*S.T.*, II-II, q. 57, art 2, ad 1). Here St. Thomas places a limit to the right of that which is proper to a person.

> require many things of others. Although our demands obviously derive from a spirit alien to virtue, and tend to ends totally lacking in humanity, they are generally recognised as just and are susceptible to the force of right, even when applied by State tribunals.[159]

There are in fact many actions which cannot be forbidden by State legislation. In the face of such laws, these actions can and must be considered as lawful or rather presumed to be such, and therefore taken as apt to serve as subject to rights.

259. The same may be said about all limited legislation. If an action is considered in special relationship with such legislation, it will not be seen as forbidden. It will, therefore, possess the character of *relative* lawfulness, even though in regard to universal legislation it may be considered unlawful. By 'universal legislation' I mean the complex of all laws obligating human beings.

260. This restricted manner of considering the *lawfulness* necessary to render an action subject to right cannot be faulted. Sometimes indeed it is necessary, when for example we have to speak of rights relative to special legislation. However, it is also the duty of writers on natural right to point out that these are not rights in the full, absolute sense of the word. It would also be highly desirable to avoid all equivocation by calling, for example, 'civil rights' those which have as their subject actions permitted and safeguarded by civil laws. The use of the adjective in this and similar cases would be very helpful.

261. It could also happen that an action seems subject to my right not because it is *per se* lawful, but because it cannot be impeded by the persons with whom I live. No one, in fact, can impede my action if I do not enter within the sphere of their rights, and I can indeed perform blameworthy actions which do not offend the rights of others. For example, if I refuse to do good to another, I am not thereby violating the sphere of rights of third persons to whom I do no harm. Consequently, it is often said that I have the right to act in this way.

But language of this kind is inexact. It is not true that I have the right to be inhuman to other people, although it is true that

[159] §11.

I have the right not to be disturbed or damaged in what I am doing if I refuse to do to others the good to which I am held by a higher moral law. In a word, 'others do not have the right to attack me, and in fact are obliged not to do so.' Nevertheless, by acting against humanity and charity, I am not exercising a right in a true, absolute sense because I am doing something which is forbidden me by the law of the Creator.

Article 6.
The fifth element: the moral exigency in other intelligent beings requiring them not to interfere with the exercise of this faculty

262. Finally, *right* implies a relationship with other intelligent beings according to which they remain morally obliged not to disturb the exercise of that faculty or moral activity. In this way the faculty, activity or action acquires the characteristic of *governance*, as we have called it. The person possessing this characteristic can justly maintain that he has been injured or offended by those who disturb or ruin it.

Article 7.
The limitation of rights is a corollary of its five constitutive elements

263. The limits within which the use of this governance is restricted, and outside which it cannot exist, depend upon the five constitutive elements of right. Later on, we shall describe these limits in detail because they alone render possible the co-existence of rights in persons sharing a common way of life. These limits are not the result of this common way of life, as we shall see, but depend upon the lack of one or other of the five elements which we have indicated as constitutive of right.

264. We must note carefully that the duty of respecting moral freedom in others does not depend upon this faculty's being a right, but on its being a right because others have the duty to respect it. It is also true that there could be in others a duty to

respect some part of the activity in a given individual without its becoming an absolute right for him. This would be the case if a part of the activity lacked one of the preceding conditions, especially that of morality.

For a person's activity to be given the status of right, it is not sufficient that the activity be morally free or, if not morally free, that it be the object of the moral duty of respect from others. Neither of these two things is enough of itself to permit this; both are necessary together. The activity of which we are speaking must be morally free on the part of the person who lays claim to the right and morally inviolable on the part of other persons who have to deal with him if he is to have this right.

265. On the other hand, we should not believe that the moral duty of respecting a portion of personal activity ceases in others if this portion is not morally free. If the moral duty of respecting the activity of others arose from a preceding right in the activity, it could be correctly inferred that the moral duty of respect ceased with the right, the object of respect. This is what many legal theorists and many publicists believe. But according to me this is one of those pernicious, profound and long-standing errors which impede the great progress to which modern legislations are called and stimulated by our present need to develop civilisation.

266. The moral freedom of some given activity in a person and the moral duty of others to respect that activity arise from different sources. The first can certainly exist without the second, and the second without the first. Infinite, unjust claims result on both sides if these two things have to proceed together, with each strictly relative to and conditioned by the other. The ensuing dispute can never be disentangled, and ends in war.

267. Let me offer examples of three classes of unjust claims which unfortunately arise every day from the error which we have described.

1st. Persons who know they have a given, morally free activity claim that this should be upheld for them by everyone else. They do not acknowledge that others sometimes have the right to impose limits to their freedom. Their excess consists in claiming immoderate freedom.

2nd. Persons who see that others have a moral duty to respect some given activity of theirs claim that this is sufficient for them to have a right, even if their activity is not morally free. This false claim emboldens people in doing evil. They decide they have the right to do it as soon as they see in others the duty not to constrain them to abandon it.

These two classes of disastrous claims are seen in those who suppose they possess some right. The third class of claims is aroused in others who have some contact with them.

3rd. Persons who see that some given activity possessed by another is not morally free and hence cannot be subject to right in the one who does it claim they are dispensed from the moral duty of respecting that activity. This claim overthrows society by creating a false equality authorising the poor to despoil the avaricious rich who give no alms. But the poor person is not morally free to do this, and therefore has no true right to it.[160]

Article 8.
Jural duty

268. We call *jural duty* that moral duty which obliges human beings to respect the freedom of others when this freedom has all the characteristics necessary to constitute a right. *Jural duty* is, therefore, the obligation that one human being has relative to the *right* of others. In other words, it is the duty which requires one human being to respect, without interference or damage, the jural governance of another. And this *jural duty* is the same as the fifth constitutive element of right.

Article 9.
Examination of the definitions given by Kant and Romagnosi

269. Various authors posit other requirements for rights, such as the joint presence of duty and right in the same person, and the state of society, but we cannot agree with them. We will discuss their opinion later. For the moment we want to concentrate our attention on drawing together all the elements required

160 The avaricious rich person has no right to abuse his riches. Nevertheless he has a right to his wealth and a right not to be deprived of it.

for constituting a right and for providing a more explicit definition of it. We say, therefore:

'Right is a personal faculty or governance, which must not be harmed, for enjoying through action or experience a lawful good.' This definition can also be called the principle of the science of right.

Authors on Right seem to pay least attention to the mutual occurrence of the twofold moral character of right, that is, to the lawfulness of the action on the part of the subject, and to the moral duty, on the part of other persons in relationship with the subject, of respecting that action. They also neglect the independence of these two characteristics. The most modern trend of thought about the concept of right is summarised in the formulas offered by Kant and Romagnosi. We must examine them briefly.

270. Kant defines right as 'the faculty of carrying out all those actions whose execution, although universal, does not impede the co-existence of other persons.' We have already examined the serious deficiencies of this formula when applied to morality.[161] Here we add only a few comments:

1. If right is made to consist in the possibility of co-existence between persons, the moral element of *lawfulness* in the action is not sufficiently emphasised. There could be some other action, unlawful according to a law of nature, which nevertheless does not exclude the co-existence of others who also commit it. But no one would have the right to such an action. The right to do evil does not exist.

2. Even if all possible unlawful actions excluded effective co-existence, they would not be unlawful simply because they produced this effect. In this case, excluding co-existence would not be constitutive of either their lawfulness or their right, but would be at most a sign by which to recognise them, a *principle of knowledge*, not a *principle of being*.

3. *Universality* itself is not a moral element, but at most an indication of the moral element. Moreover, it is a highly equivocal indication, in great need of interpretation. We could be speaking either of absolute universality or of universality relative to

[161] Cf. *Storia Comparativa e Critica de' sistemi morali*, c. 5, art. 11.

the circumstances of the person doing the action. In the first case, any lawful action, if done by all human beings, would exclude co-existence. If everyone decided to be a shoemaker, who would farm the land? In the second case, no evil action would exclude co-existence, though everyone could do it in the same circumstances, because the same circumstances would never be repeated, or very rarely.

4. Finally, it cannot be said that an action, if certainly lawful without excluding co-existence, must by this very fact be left free by other people (this is a required condition if the action is to be called a right). In fact, a father, by means of his paternal right, can impede even the most lawful of his child's actions though these actions, considered as a whole, do not exclude co-existence. These actions of the child, relative to the father, cannot therefore merit the title of true *right*.[162]

271. Romagnosi offers this definition: right is 'the power of a human being to act without impediment in accordance with the law of nature, and to obtain from others that which is due to him by force of the law itself.'[163]

There are several reasons for not admitting this definition of right.

1. It is not the definition of right in general. It seems insufficient to say, 'the faculty for acting in accordance with the law of nature.' If this way of speaking has to be followed, it would be better to say, 'in accordance with the law', without restriction. In this case, the affirmation could be applied to any law whatsoever, natural or positive, without fear of defining abstract right —

[162] Kant's formula was reproduced in Italy (cf. Dr. Pietro Bartoli, *Diritto naturale*, p. 1, sect. 1, c. 1). I should add that many authors on right do not distinguish carefully the state of simple co-existence between human beings and the state of society. The notion of right must be independent of the state of society; right exists between two individuals of the human species who may not have formed any society between themselves. Almost all modern authors on natural right, as well as some Italian writers, err by making society part of the general definition of right. We, however, exclude from the notion of right in general not only the concept of society, but also that of any *real* co-existence. Possible co-existence alone is sufficient. In other words, we maintain that the idea of right would exist even if there were only one individual of the human species, provided this individual were considered in hypothetical relationship with other possible beings like him.

[163] *Assunto primo*, §3.

which is not true, effective right. I realise that Romagnosi will say that he intended to define *natural right*. I would reply that if an action were to be prohibited by a positive, obligating law, that action would automatically cease to be a true *right of nature*. From the moment of its prohibition, it would cease to be a right of any sort.

We have to abandon these abstractions in which the science of right has gone so far astray. They generate a maze of inextricable problems harmful to mankind. Who would not say 'No' to the question, 'Can a person's right be *impeded* by the positive law?' Nevertheless, positive law makes unlawful certain naturally free actions. What we have to say is that positive law does not put any impediment to the exercise of natural rights, but does make some of these rights cease altogether by eliminating one of the conditions required for the actions to be rights. This condition is the total moral lawfulness of these actions.

2. Saying, 'the power for acting according to the law of nature', supposes that the law of nature regulates all actions. But there are actions which in themselves are indifferent, that is, neither commanded nor forbidden by the law of nature. However, simple *permission*, although sometimes called an act of positive law, does not seem to be an act of the law of nature. This law refers to what is *lawful*, not to what is *permitted*. And the only condition for lawfulness here is inaction on the part of the natural law. Whoever does what is merely lawful, acts relatively to that about which the natural law is silent and provides no norm.

3. In the affirmation, 'the power to act without impediment according to natural law', the nature of the impediment remains unknown. If the obstacle is physical and independent of other human beings, the right is not removed. If the obstacle has been placed by others, we still have to distinguish, because that obstacle could have been placed justly or unjustly as a bar to our *per se* lawful action. If the obstacle to our *per se* lawful action is altogether unjust, our right is injured but still subsists, although we no longer have unfettered power to act. If, however, the obstacle placed by others is just, we would not have the right even if they did not posit the obstacle. Our action loses its characteristic of right even if it is only *possible* for others to posit the obstacle justly. — In the same way, when we say 'the

power to act', it is not clear if the power in question is moral or physical. If the meaning is, 'a physical power for acting in accordance with the natural law without any physical impediment', no right would be constituted. The definition, therefore, is highly ambiguous.

4. Introducing into the definition the words 'that which is due to him' seems the same as introducing what has been defined into the definition. The only explanation of 'what is due to him' is 'that to which he has a right.'

5. Again, in saying 'the power to obtain', etc., we do not know if the reference is to physical or moral power. In the first case, no *right* would be present. But even if the physical power were impeded, the right could be present, although the person concerned would not be able *to obtain* that which is his due. *Obtaining* or not obtaining what is due is a factual circumstance which does not alter the nature of the right. We can have a right to try to obtain forcefully what is ours without necessarily obtaining it.

6. In saying 'the power to act' and then 'the power to obtain', right is needlessly split into two powers. First, 'the power to act' is so general an expression that it includes even the power to obtain, and every other power. This addition, therefore, is useless repetition. Again, 'the faculty to obtain', that is, to employ coercion in order to have what is our own, must be dealt with as a particular function of right. Otherwise, it would be impossible to assign a limit to this function. If having a right to something implied the power to obtain it without condition, I could use any means I liked to obtain it because the person who possesses a right has a right to the means. But as we shall see, a great number of means cannot be used even for the just end of obtaining what is our own. If we lack upright, lawful means, we have to renounce the exercise of our right. As far as exercising it is concerned, our right would cease.

Romagnosi's definition is, therefore, imprecisely expressed, and contains many substantial errors.

272. Finally, it is, I believe, altogether necessary to abandon the system of those authors who in their treatises on right maintain that we can prescind from the divinity. If this primary relationship is rejected, morally unlawful actions are easily elevated to the status of rights because they do not enter, as we said,

into other people's sphere of rights. Scientifically considered, such abstractions are totally frivolous. Considered in their logical consequences, they are sources of error; considered in their real effects, they are very harmful to the human race.

273. No activity therefore can have the quality of right, and consequently be a true *right*, unless it is lawful in the sight of the whole moral law. A prohibited action can indeed be called a *relative right*, and will be such if we consider it (here we sum up):

1. either in relationship with some special legislation — in this case, it is a right relative only to this legislation;[164]
2. or in relationship to the judgment of people who in certain cases cannot judge of its immorality and hence are bound to presume its uprightness —*presumed right*;
3. or in relationship to the obligation that others have of not impeding it, although it is unlawful — *unrefined right*.[165]

A right does not cease to be absolute in the possession of the person who has a just title to it, even when he abuses that right. Abuse on its own remains outside the sphere of right, and it is only the abuse of right which can be impeded.

[164] For example, State tribunals, which have to judge according to established laws, would violate this kind of *relative right* if they condemned a guilty person who according to the laws ought to have been acquitted, even though he were truly guilty of the accusation.

[165] For example, I would violate the right of a fellow human being if I impeded the practice of his false religion, which he thinks is true, without first convincing him of the falsity and unlawfulness of that religion. He has the right (when he does no harm to others) to act in accordance with his persuasions. Persuasion cannot be forced, but changed only by way of peaceful argument. Nevertheless, his right is only *relative* to the duty that I have to respect his actions, although they are unlawful. This is what I call *unrefined right*.

CHAPTER 3
The relationship between right and duty

Article 1.
In the human being the notion of *duty* precedes that of *right*

274. If right is a moral governance enabling us to do what is not forbidden but protected by law, the notion of *duty* necessarily precedes, and is independent of that of *right*. If, on the other hand, the notion of duty did not come first, either the notion of right would have to be one of the first, self-evident notions, or it would be totally impossible for us to form it.

275. The notion of right is necessarily included in that of duty, as we can see from the definition I have given. But if the notion of right is explained by a notion of duty which does not precede that of right, the definition will be defective because it begs the question. Many authors have in fact defined right in this way; they have said that the notions of right and duty are essentially relative, so that one includes the other. As a result the notions have become obscure and unintelligible (we cannot explain one by means of the other), and the deduction of duties and rights arbitrary. Such a way of thinking implies that on the one hand human beings have a right to do anything not forbidden by duty, and on the other that duty does not forbid human beings from doing what they have a right to do. This perpetual circle provides only an arbitrary principle of what is upright and just.

276. In my teaching, duty has its own existence and precedes that of right in human beings. Duty is imposed by the *object*, whereas right, relative to its matter, springs from the *subject*. Just as the object has an existence independent of the human subject, so duty has an existence independent of right.[166]

[166] I am talking here about the priority of duty relative to human beings. In God the notions of duty and right take on a more noble aspect and change nature. However, we can say that in God there is something that corresponds to moral responsibility (if not duty), and something that corresponds to right, but without any real precedence between the two. Indeed in the divine persons *charity* is *moral responsibility*. But charity itself is essential to God and the fullness of God; St. John says that 'God is charity'. Again, charity is

Article 2.
The notion of duty is simple; that of right, complex

277. It follows from this, and from what has been said earlier, that the notion of *duty*, which does not involve right, is simpler than the notion of *right*, which involves duty. This explains why many people have clear ideas about duty but not about the notion of right.[167]

Article 3.
A right does not correspond to every duty, but duties correspond to every right

278. We can now see also how *duties* can exist without any corresponding rights.[168] To feel ourselves bound by a duty, it is sufficient that an intellective nature present itself to us. This perception alone requires us not to be unjust to such a nature, not to judge it falsely; in other words we must acknowledge and respect the degree of *entity* in which it shares.

The first duties, at least considered abstractly, are not to any given person but to impersonal *truth*. Truth, as something infinite, renders the person an object to be respected. Only the

the total action of God because there is no distinction in him between physical and moral power; every physical power is moral, every action of God is charity. Thus the whole of his action is simultaneously responsible and jural; it is responsibility and inalienable right. If the divine action is considered in relationship to creatures, the same must be said, that is, his action can always be considered as a responsibility and an essential right.

[167] Children very easily acquire the idea of *duty* but not that of right. The wise authoress of *Lettres de famille sur l'éducation* observes: 'The idea of right is complex. It is composed of the twofold position of the contracting parties. The idea of *duty* is one, its origin is beyond our investigation, and its expression allows no response; "You must" has to be accepted without comment. Examining right tires the lively attention and sluggish intelligence of children, while the security of *duty* satisfies their preference for decisions, and their need for the support of authority. When allowed their own choice, they often ask us what to do. Our "Do what you like" meets with "What am I to do?"; they are looking for some kind of duty, or at least authority, in their uncertainty' (*Lett*., 44).

[168] We could also say that inherent to every duty is 'the right to fulfil it.'

infinite ennobles intelligent beings by furnishing them with their nature as ends[169] and thus making them susceptible of rights.

279. Furthermore, when I consider myself objectively, I have duties to myself and must respect my own personal dignity. Here again there are no rights corresponding to duties, because rights towards oneself are mentally inconceivable.

280. The duties which we each have to impersonal truth and the duties to our own personship are absolute, and do not involve any relationship with other human beings or persons. Hence rights corresponding to these kinds of duties do not exist (except in God seen as the moral law); they can only exist in other persons, whose existence is not necessary for the existence of these duties.

On the other hand, no right can exist in us unless the duty to respect it exists in others, as we have seen.

Article 4.
Right is generated by duty: the manner of this generation

281. Duty therefore generates right.

Duties, it was claimed in the last century, are derived from rights rather than rights from duties. This lethal teaching was the result of inhuman selfishness. Our century proclaims the opposite,[170] the only true, human teaching, which we have an obligation to explain and clarify.

[169] Cf. *PE*, 101–105.

[170] Mme. Guizot, wife of a well-known minister of state, is a case in point. She writes: 'The idea of duty must precede that of right, just as cause precedes effect. Rights exist because duties exist, not vice versa, just as society exists because human beings exist and not vice versa. All social rights bestowed on us by our human nature are ours by virtue of the duties owed to us by other human beings, our equals. A father has the right to the obedience of his son as long as obedience is the son's duty. When the duty has ceased, the right no longer exists; the father's nature is still the same, only the son's has changed. The source of the father's right over his son no longer exists because obedience is no longer a duty. In every society right presupposes duty; the authority of laws is founded on the duty to observe them. If a human being

282. *Duty* generates right by two acts: one relative to the person who acquires a right, the other relative to the other persons who must respect this right.

Duty, relative to the person acquiring right, limits his personal activity within defined limits, which constitute the sphere of right.

Relative to other persons, duty obliges them to respect personal activity, whose limits are determined by the duty itself of the person who possesses the activity. It is principally this act of duty which raises that portion of activity to the dignity of right, rendering it sacred and inviolable.

283. Right therefore is a power which, relative to its possessor, is *upright* and, relative to others, is *inviolable*.

Moral duty renders right *upright* by restricting it *negatively*, that is, by prescribing its limits. Moral duty also renders right *inviolable*, by acting *positively*, that is, by obliging others to respect right within those limits. Properly speaking this second positive action of duty gives right its form; right is right because it is inviolable. Right would not exist if other persons did not first have the duty of leaving intact the portion of power or activity called right.

284. To know therefore the sphere of rights of a human being, we must first consider his duties. By doing this we find the portion of activity that is morally free for him. But we must also consider the duties of the persons with whom he is in relationship to see the obligations they have to respect this portion of activity, because only that part of the whole portion can correctly be called right which, relative to other persons, is rendered inviolable by their duty.

285. The failure to consider that a negative act of duty comes before right, gave rise to the absurd, monstrous and so-called right to do what is wrong. Right however originates through the obligation to respect upright activity, an obligation imposed on other persons by the subject of right. The same kind of

lived among wolves, we would not speak of mutual rights, but simply of a fact. The man would not punish a wolf that took his sheep because the wolf had violated his right to ownership; he would not recognise any duty of the wolf to respect his right. He would simply attack the animal and kill it to regain his property' (*Lett.*, 44).

reasoning gave rise to opinions asserting that the only source of rights in human beings is society, or at least real association between human beings. These and similar errors have already been dealt with.

Article 5.
Duty is expressed negatively; right, positively

286. Another important relationship between duty and right is the way in which they are expressed; the former is expressed negatively, the latter positively.

As we have seen, duty directly determines the *mode* of being of our actions in order to make them conform with the law. Duty therefore is first expressed negatively: it prohibits and does not command; it prohibits our practical judgment from giving things greater or lesser value than they appear to us to merit. In fact law, in its first expression, does not require us to reflect on things and judge them. This would be impossible because law begins to propagate itself and command us only at the moment we reflect on things.

287. On the other hand, everything not forbidden by such law may be freely done by us, and forms our right as soon as the duty of respecting our freedom arises in others. Thus the first expression of right has a positive, not a negative form: it *permits*, it does not *prohibit*.

288. We can see therefore that authors often express themselves equivocally, with great confusion of ideas when they maintain that Right admits only *negative*, perfect duties, and that morals recognises *positive* but imperfect duties. Instead of this, we should consider the science of right as dealing solely with rights, although in relationship with certain duties, and the science of morality must be considered as dealing solely with duties and responsibilities, although in relationship with rights. Thus all rights are positive, while duties can be either positive or negative. Duties that have a relationship with rights can always be reduced to the following general, negative formula: 'Do not diminish the good of another' or equivalently, 'Do no harm'.

Article 6.
The obligatory part of actions appertains to duty; the lawful part to right

289. Duty therefore concerns that to which we are obligated [*App*., no. 2]. Right on the other hand can extend to the whole sphere of non-prohibited actions, provided they do not lack the other constitutives of right we have mentioned. When I say 'non-prohibited actions', I mean those actions that are simply lawful. These can be divided into three classes: 1. simply *lawful* actions, 2. lawful and *obligatory* actions, 3. lawful, non-obligatory actions enhanced by special moral goodness, that is, *supererogatory* actions. All these three classes can be the matter of right.

290. It is clear that an action, if obligatory, is by its nature the matter of an absolute, inalienable right. I will return to this kind of right when I deduce and classify special rights.

Non-obligatory actions endowed with moral goodness are such that moral perfection depends upon them. We are in fact free to do them or omit them, or do them to a certain extent, and thus attain various degrees of *goodness* according to the good we do. Just as *justice* precedes and generates right, right precedes and generates *goodness*, which consists precisely in using our own right to do good to others. We perfect ourselves morally in proportion to the good we have, and to the extent that we are authors of good. Hence degrees of goodness, relative to the person who has goodness, are called degrees of *moral perfection*. *Goodness* towards other human beings is called *beneficence*; towards God, *piety*.

Finally, merely lawful actions, devoid of obligation and moral goodness, can also be matter for right. When considered in themselves as abstract conceptions, such actions can indeed be called 'indifferent', that is, devoid of both malice and moral goodness. Obviously they can never be entirely indifferent, as moralists generally teach, when they are considered in the individual who carries them out. In such a case these actions are accompanied by all the circumstances present or added by the person who does them (the person's intention, for instance, is a major factor).[171]

[171] The Council of Constance (sect. 17) condemned John Hus' 16th article,

291. We have to speak about these actions understood abstractly because the teaching on rights cannot be considered in any other way. Such teaching must indicate not only when a right exists in an individual, but also when other human beings must judge it to exist in the individual; the action must be considered in the individual no less than in itself. Considering the action in the individual helps us to establish when right truly exists or not; considering it in itself helps us to establish, generally speaking, those occasions when others must judge (presume) that the right exists. I will explain.

292. Let us take an action which in itself is indifferent, but blameworthy in the person doing it because of his evil intention or because of some accidental addition. We can now ask two questions:

1. Has he the right to do it?
2. Must I judge that he has the right to do it?

We say 'No' to the first question, 'Yes' to the second, for the following reasons:

If we suppose that the intention of the person doing the action is evil and that consequently his action is evil, he certainly cannot have any right to do it: nobody has the right to posit evil acts. But, because I cannot know the intention with full certainty, the circumstance rendering the action evil (that is, the evil intention of the person doing it) cannot be subjected to my judgment — unless the author's confession and other definite, external proofs have revealed it. I can only apply my judgment to the action considered in itself. In this case I must judge that it can indeed be suitable matter for the right in question, and that the person has a right to do it. Hence I must base my conduct on this principle, and respect in others what we have called elsewhere 'presumed right'.[172]

'There are no indifferent actions.' The proposition must be understood as condemned relative to actions considered in themselves, in their species, not in the individual positing them.

[172] Note that if a subjective circumstance (for example, an evil intention) renders an action evil, the right that can be present in the action, considered in itself, may still remain available for the individual. However the person, when performing the action, has no right to add to it the circumstance or evil intention which renders it culpable.

CHAPTER 4
The nature and extension of jural duty

293. We now have to clarify the nature and extension of the moral duty that corresponds to right. We have called this 'jural duty'.

Article 1.
The nature of jural obligation

§1. *Definition*

294. First, we must define the nature of jural obligation on the basis of what we have said. 'Jural obligation is that moral duty which obliges one person to leave intact and free some activity proper to another person.' All the parts of this definition are clarified by what has been said except for the final phrase, in which it is affirmed that the activity constituting the subject of right must be *proper* to another person, that is, to a person different from the one who has the obligation.

We have not in fact explained the concept of 'proper to', although we all know more or less distinctly what we mean by it. For the moment, therefore, we shall make use of the knowledge which everyone has, and which reveals itself very early in children. The concept will be developed more at length in its own place. Our present aim is to draw the principal qualities or conditions of jural obligation from the definition we have given.

§2. *Two species of jural obligation: one arising from the nature of the activity which forms the object of the jural obligation, the other from an extraneous cause*

295. Our definition shows first that we do not expect as a condition of jural obligation that the definition proceed immediately from the capacity for respect inherent in the activity

(right) that forms its object. The obligation we call 'jural' does not disturb or impede that activity even if the obligation itself arises from an extraneous cause rather than from the moral exigency of the activity itself.

296. For example, a workman who owes his employer ten hours of work a day may obtain permission to rest until he is called to work. In this case, he possesses governance over his time as long as the employer permits. But what is the source of the jural duty now existing in other people which requires them not to impede the use of his free time? It does not appear to come from the faculty that the employee has for labouring for his own profit. The faculty of which we are speaking belongs to the employer and was provided by the employer for the workman's benefit. It comes therefore from the permission granted by the employer himself. Respect is due to a right of the employer which has passed to the employee. We can say that in these circumstances employer and employee form as it were a single person whose faculty is not to be violated by anyone.[173]

297. There exist, therefore, some faculties for acting morally which draw in their wake the jural duty to be respected. They do this, however, not *per se* but as a result of some accident or relationship that envelops them.

298. It is true that this teaching could be expressed in another way by distinguishing between the activity taken materially and the activity furnished with all the circumstances and qualities which render it jural and worthy of respect. It could be maintained (if the activity of which we are speaking is to be taken in all its jural-moral extension and not in its material entity) that 'every jural obligation has its foundation (its reason) in the faculty that forms its object.'

Often enough, though, such a way of speaking is awkward. It is more convenient to divide jural obligations into two classes, that is:

1. *The class of jural obligations* which arise from the exigency of the activity that forms its immediate object, without need to appeal to anything from which it may be derived.

[173] The worker's right to rest can also be considered as a *transmitted* right, not as a right *subsisting* of itself. We shall speak later of the *transmission of rights*.

2. *The class of jural obligations* that do not arise from the exigency of a single activity — the exigency forming the immediate object of the activity — but from a person other than the one to whom the faculty pertains.

Both ways of speaking seem exact to me but needed to be distinguished and identified for the sake of clarity. The reader is now in a position to interpret both correctly when we have to use them.

§3. *Jural obligation is always related to other persons*

299. Obligation may belong to the first or the second of the two classes we have indicated, but in both cases one of its properties is that it always refers to a person different from the one in whom it is found.

Certainly it is possible for me to have duties towards myself provided I consider myself objectively.[174] But my duties towards myself, although *moral*, cannot be called *jural* because no one can have *rights* in his own regard. The word 'jural' has its root in *jus*, and hence is equivalent to 'duty corresponding to a right', or better 'informing a right.' All jural duties are indeed moral, but not all moral duties are jural. Moral, jural duties have as their object the need to respect, that is, not to remove or harm, some activity proper to another person.

The fact that corresponding rights and jural duties exist between different persons and never in the same person, makes conflict possible between two persons in the case of usurpation or harm on one side, and revendication and compensation on the other. The possibility of this conflict misled many authors, who were persuaded that *de facto* coercion is essential to every right.

[174] The phrase 'duties towards ourselves' is not altogether exact, as I noted in *PE*, 215–227. The word 'ourselves' expresses a *subject*, and there are no duties towards *subject* as *subject*. We ought to substitute for 'ourselves' the phrase, 'duties towards that human being who is *ourselves*', but this would grate on literary susceptibility which is often contemptuous of new ways of speaking.

§4. *Not all moral duties towards another person are jural; only those which command respect for an activity proper to that person*

300. The sphere of jural duties is further restricted if we consider the five elements which we have accepted as constitutive of the notion of right. A moral duty can be a jural obligation only if it both terminates in another person and has for its object the activity of that other person.

§5. *The negative sense of jural obligations*

301. It is clear, therefore, that of its nature jural obligation is negative. It requires us not to harm and not to attempt to harm what is proper to others. Nevertheless, we have to show clearly how this negative form is constituted. This we can do by means of the following observations.

302. First, jural duty forbids *de facto* injury, and any attempt to do injury, to another's faculty. Consequently harm can be done to the right of the supreme Being, though the faculties and properties of this Being cannot be limited or damaged. A person who neglects to carry out some act of benevolence imposed by the Creator does not damage any jural duty towards human beings, but is guilty relative to the supreme Legislator who has the right to impose the precept and require its fulfilment. On the other hand, the duties of benevolence and beneficence, if considered as imposed by the light of reason alone without reference to the supreme Legislator, cannot be called jural duties because they neither impede others in the exercise of their own activity, nor attempt to harm them. In this way two disparate opinions are reconciled.

303. Another reconciliation of different opinions may be carried out here. Thomasius posited as the foundation of Right (1705) the precept of Christian morality:[175] 'Do not do to others what you do not want done to yourself.' His corollary — that

[175] Note how the principal authors always fall back, consciously or unconsciously, on a moral principle as the source from which to derive the science of right.

the duties of right are negative — justifiably encountered strong opposition, as we noted.

More recently, Romagnosi maintained that 'the separation made by Thomasius is absurd in the extreme, disastrous and destructive of sociality.' He was led to this conclusion because society itself is required by natural right and demands positive mutual assistance.[176] We need not insist, however, on the way in which Thomasius conceived jural duty as negative. I maintain that Romagnosi's positive jural duties can be reduced to duties of a negative form.

In fact, the negative duty of right prescribes: 'Do not harm others', while Romagnosi requires that 'human beings associate amongst themselves and offer one another the necessary assistance to prevent the loss and suffering of each individual.' The positive duties that Romagnosi claims to introduce into natural Right are therefore reduced to a special class of negative duties. In other words, they are reduced to the duty of not causing harm to others. It is true that it is sometimes necessary to offer help to others in order to avoid causing them harm, as we shall see later (Thomasius was aware of this). But what Romagnosi added is only a means of carrying out the general negative rule that we must not cause harm to others. This is why I said that 'the general form of jural duties is negative,' although these duties can sometimes take a special, positive form. However, they will always be reduced to the negative form, which is their primitive, general form.

§6. *The external aspect of jural duty*

304. We now have to ask if jural duty is an external duty. We

[176] Romagnosi is correct when he says: 'If human beings were either God or beasts, and hence self-sufficient, as Aristotle said, any social state would be purely a matter of choice and Thomasius' principle could be defended. But if some social state is absolutely necessary as a means (as it is), it follows that all the positive duties of security and assistance form part of necessary natural Right in the same way as negative duties' (*Raguaglio storico e statistico degli studi di Diritto Germanico e naturale in Allemagna*, in the preface to the *Assunto Primo*, etc., Florence, 1832). — Romagnosi's affirmation is basically true, but exaggerated. Later we shall try to restrict it to its proper limits.

begin by noting that the word 'external' is ambiguous. If it is to be retained in a treatise on right, therefore, it must be rigorously defined and its meaning limited.

In its initial meaning *externality* is a property of bodies in which every particle is assignable outside all others. The proper meaning of externality and its derivatives is not applicable, therefore, to moral duties which are neither bodies, nor parts of bodies but pertain to the order of spiritual and suprasensible things. Moral duty, which lacks the relationships expressed in the words 'internal' and 'external' cannot be called internal or external. But could the *object* of moral duty be external?

305. The word 'external' involves a relationship with something else outside. But what is that thing relative to which the object of moral duty is said to be external? Is it our body, in the sense that the object of moral duty may be understood as external to our own body? In this case, we may be talking about the *material object* of duty, and here there is no doubt that moral duty can be referred to an object external to our body such as life or other people's belongings which, materially understood, are objects external to our body. But we may also be talking about the *formal object* of duty which is constituted by the relationship that the object has with the law. In this relationship, which is not a material relationship in the sense that 'external' or 'internal' can be applied to it, the law determines what has to be done or not done[177] in the object's regard. Life and other people's belongings, taken materially, are not yet the proper, true, immediate object of obligation.

The immediate object of obligation is 'carrying out the law', that is, the execution of what the law prescribes relative to the object, which may be material or not. If we want to use philosophically appropriate language, we cannot say that any moral duty has an external object, but we can say that the moral law prescribes something to be done or omitted relative to an object external to our body.

306. However, if we want to keep in touch with our ordinary manner of speaking, we can call jural duty 'external' provided we take the word in a translated sense, as we normally do. In this

[177] For the distinction between the *physical, intellectual* and *moral* object of duty, cf. *CS*, 597–599.

case, it does not indicate true externality, but the relationship, involved in such a duty, between the person whose duty it is and the person who has the activity (the right) which is the object of the duty, because duty requires this activity to be respected. John's activity, which I must respect, is said to be outside me in some way because it resides in someone different from me. My duty, therefore, which terminates in that person, is said metaphorically to terminate in an external object.

307. The violation of a right involves the kind of externality which could be described as *otherness*. In fact, I cannot offend the proper activity of another person unless my action causes harm or attempts to cause harm to that activity. My blameworthy act, therefore, has an effect related to a person different from myself whom I either actually harm, or want and attempt to harm.

The observance of such a duty is normally a non-act. Thus, this kind of externality is verified only in the transgression, not the observance of jural duty. In transgressing our duty we act positively.

308. Sins against our neighbours, therefore, when they are entirely internal to the spirit, without any outward effect or sign and unaccompanied by an attempt to harm, cannot properly be called violations of our jural duties towards their rights. Our acts in this case lack the kind of externality which is required to constitute such violations. But we cannot say the same about our relationship with the supreme Being; relative to him all our sins have the nature of true lesions of right, simply because there is nothing hidden or internal as far as this Being is concerned. He is the truth, the essence of being. Every lie and every disordered act of ours is consequently an assault on his very essence. Everything exists in him, even the spirit of the sinner. The disorder effected by the sinner in himself is, therefore, an assault on what essentially *belongs* to God who governs being, all of which comes from him as its principle and receives from him its every act.[178]

[178] The word 'justice' was first employed by Christianity to indicate the fulfilment of all duties, *omnium mandatorum custodia*, as St. John Chrysostom defined it (Hom. 12 *in Matt.*). The reason for this new use of the word is that Christianity re-united the human creature with the Creator, and called

Article 2.
The extension of jural duty

309. From what has been said, we can also draw some conclusions about the extension of jural duty. This we will do now. The reader already knows that I disapprove of the method followed by writers who intend to restrict the teaching on rights simply to relationships between human beings. It seems obvious to me that the science of right can never be considered complete and perfect until the rights of the first Being are taken into account together with the jural duties which correspond to them.

310. But we could ask whether the part of the science of right that deals with mere relationships between human beings is sufficiently independent of the consideration of the rights of the supreme Being to be treated fully enough, and without error, when these divine rights are omitted from the argument. The

human beings to consider the morality of their actions in relationship with the principle of their actions. This relationship embraces the fullness of morality. Christ, in fulfilling morality and raising it to a supernatural level, said: 'Blessed are they who hunger and thirst after *justice*' (Matt 5: [6, Douai]). With a single word, he pointed out the whole of virtue and perfection. Previously we said that many works of beneficence, which are not obligatory considered relative to the relationship between human beings, become obligatory considered in relationship to God. Consequently, charity itself, the greatest precept under the law of the gospel, forms justice in the Christian system, that is, perfect virtue in the eyes of God. St. Augustine commented so aptly on this sublime teaching: 'The charity of God which alone makes just whoever is just' (*De Nat. et gr.*, c. 38). Again, 'Incipient charity is incipient justice; great charity is great justice; perfect charity is perfect justice' (*ibid.*, last chap.). — Natural reason had come to know that the word *justum* expressed etymologically the concept of equality and had come to mean 'that which is on a par or commensurate with the rule to which it must be on a par or commensurate', as Aristotle himself noted (cf. *Eth.* 1). But revealed reason added that 'this rule, with which actions have to be commensurate in order to be just, is the divine will, which itself has been clearly communicated to human beings.' From then on the word 'just' was used to describe the perfect human being, and 'justice' to indicate 'the perfection resulting from the complex of all virtues.' This was the sublime, noble meaning found on the lips of all and in every language of the universe. In this way the value of words used by human beings is changed and clarified as greater light is bestowed upon mankind.

solution to such a question depends on the teaching about the morality of right.

311. We have shown that there is no true, complete right, whatever its source, which can be immoral. Immorality, by adhering to a right, destroys it. With this in mind, the question can be answered without difficulty: even the rights that people have amongst themselves cannot be dealt with without taking into consideration the rights of the first Being. If human rights were to come into collision with divine rights, the former would cease to be rights because they would *ipso facto* be rendered immoral.

312. At one time, divine rights were abstracted from consideration of human rights because this was thought necessary to ensure a rigorously scientific method. But this opinion was false. The best method, the truly scientific method, can never be constrained to carry out the kind of abstractions that destroy the subject under investigation and leave us with nothing more than hypothetical results which have no relevance whatsoever to practice. Practice requires us to deal with realities, not abstractions.

313. Taking the rules drawn from hypothetical and abstract data as rules for practice is sure to lead to ill-advised and very dangerous arrangements. And unfortunately this does occur. A considerable part of the imperfection and downright evil of positive laws has always been due and still is due to the abuse of rules based on the abstractions to which lawyers are so addicted.

What was first introduced into the treatise on right under the pretext of scientific method was welcomed with open arms because it was so favourable to the system embraced by modern irreligion; the irreligious were delighted to find that 'it was against the rigour of scientific method to introduce the name of God and consideration of his rights into the treatises on human rights.' Supporters of modern irreligion were equally delighted with the consequence: 'human rights exist independently of those of God' and even more with the other conclusion: 'it is not necessary to pay attention to any possible collision that could take place between rights of human beings towards one another and human rights relative to the supreme Being.' These are the deformed foundations of the politics and the human, material, irreligious legislation that my contemporaries, and those of my father, have had to contemplate. I can only hope that their children are not subjected to the same fate!

314. It may be possible, therefore, to abstain from specifying the rights of the first Being in this work, but we have to proclaim their existence, and state clearly that human rights, which are of a lower order than divine rights, are conditioned by and subordinate to divine rights. We shall, therefore, have recourse to divine rights whenever this is necessary to complete the treatise on human rights, the principal aim of this book.

315. Meanwhile, let us recall that the moral system we have explained presents four classes of duties which consist in *simple, affective, spoken and externally executed volitions.*[179] All these classes are jural duties relative to God. This is not the case relative to human beings.

316. We must note carefully, however, that even those duties which are jural relative to human beings have their root in preceding moral duties of which they are, so to speak, a continuation. Jural duties cannot be cut off from their main stem without disintegrating in our hands. For example, simple ill-will without any external effect does not contain any attempt to harm another's activity and does not, therefore, offend any human jural duty.[180] But although jural duty begins only with the attempt to do harm to another, this attempt, considered apart from the internal ill-will causing it, is not of itself the object of any jural duty. The entire seat of evil is found properly speaking in internal ill-will [*App.*, no. 3].

317. We repeat: duty cannot be split in two, one part moral and the other jural. The jural element of duty is grafted into the moral root where it attaches itself indivisibly.

179 *Words* and *material actions* could be reduced to the same class because both are material actions. We have in fact done this elsewhere. However, they can be usefully distinguished in so far as words act immediately simply by making us know something, while actions *change the state of material things.*

180 Ill-will can exist in the heart, irrespective of any actual volition intending harm of another. But if such a volition is present, it is an injury done to jural duty because it is already the principle of harm against the right of another. Nevertheless, it is not subject to coercion as long as it remains hidden in the spirit.

The general precept of natural right is: 'Give to each his right.' All natural rights without exception are ultimately reduced to this rule, and can be deduced from it as a necessary consequence
(Sam. Cocceji, *Dissert.* Prooem., 12, §51)

THE PRINCIPLE OF THE DERIVATION OF RIGHTS

THE PRINCIPLE
OF THE
DERIVATION OF RIGHTS

318. It seems to me that the time has come for writers not only to affirm what is true, but to present it more clearly by deducing one truth from another logically. Human understanding, which has generally developed in backward nations, is now set on a road from which it was for long excluded by ancient errors and traditional prejudices. Mankind, although crushed by its disastrous experiences, and consequently more mistrustful than ever of human knowledge, will rediscover its confidence if knowledge is clearly expressed through connected, logically justified ideas. Logical order is undoubtedly our best guarantee against error.

Error has in fact become more refined as mental application and sophistication have increased. The result is to arouse greater suspicion in human beings, all of whom are created for truth, and to make them insist on rigorous proofs with clear concepts and deductions. Indeed, once the human mind has savoured the beauty, efficacy and humanity of clear, distinct reasoning, it no longer accepts the burden of confused concepts, ambiguous assertions and incoherent language. Our age, like every other, has its faults, but it cannot be accused, thank God, of tolerating teachers who try to mask their ignorance behind a pretended monopoly of knowledge clothed in complex arguments and captious language.

Yes, it is indeed to be hoped that all things, human and divine, should be expressed sincerely, developed logically and accurately, and argued with precision from their simple principles. Many useless questions would then be omitted; many would change their nature and take other forms, and some would be settled as soon as stated. A little analysis introduced into discussion would put an end to the bitter debates between differing schools and other warring parties and authorities. The light of real certainty would return, agreement be reached, and presumption publicly rebutted.

319. In my own case, my sole intention is to express the little knowledge I have as best I can, and share it with others. I want to do this simply and logically, while aiming at consistent, although not necessarily conventional development; but I will not adopt the language of any particular school, nor attempt to speak *ex cathedra.* This has always been my practice, and the result is well-known — vituperation and calumny. But such things pass, and truth, my great, ineffable consolation, remains. And if I have been blessed enough to have unlocked or indicated truth for others, the way to truth will remain open.

I intend to pursue more rigorously the method that I have constantly proclaimed. Conclusions will I hope be seen in the original light of evident principles, where their truth is best demonstrated. They come to birth, as it were, from the principles, and their legitimacy cannot be doubted.

320. But what we have said needs to be applied to the present book, in which we propose to demonstrate the method to be followed by philosophers in deriving from their supreme principle, in an orderly fashion, the rights of nature and reason which apply to mankind in its mutual relationships. The previous book on the ESSENCE of right will be of assistance to us here. In fact the derivation of particular rights cannot be carried out without knowledge of the *essence* of every right (this essence, in so far as it is known, was also called by us the *notion* of right). But granted the conclusions about the notion and definition of right which result from our long discusssion of the matter, we can now apply what we know in order to derive from the principle of right all the particular rights of which human beings are capable.

It is clear that the essence of right, which must be present in each and every particular, genuine right, is the sure *rule* with which to discern when a right has been posited and when it has not. We can express this rule, if we wish, as follows: 'We judge that a right is present wherever we find the *notion* of right (which consists of the five elements we have indicated); in the absence of this notion, no right is present.' This explains why we called the *common notion* of right 'the *supreme principle* of the science of right'. The essence of things contained in their notion is such that when an essence is known it always shows us which particular things participate in it and which do not.

321. But before applying the notion of right to different human activities in order to verify which activities acquire the moral dignity that makes them rights, it will be helpful if we follow the dictates of cautious logic in the long, difficult task of verifying individual human rights, and endeavour to find some reliable rules, some faithful stars, to guide us on our journey. We will be especially helped if there is a supreme rule, the first of all rules, which we could fittingly call the *principle of the derivation of rights.* In fact, the pyramidal form (composed of different propositions, the lowest being greater in number, the highest less), in which truth is always present for contemplation by human minds, makes the existence of this principle highly probable.

We have now reached the core of this book, which I have entitled 'The principle of the derivation of rights' because it deals with this principle alone.

CHAPTER 1

Some logical rules to be born in mind in the derivation of rights

Article 1.
The distinction between *simple* and *complex* rights — The first rule

322. Our investigation must begin, I believe, with an observation about how we have to express ourselves, and first of all, about the use of the word 'right' itself. This word is sometimes (in fact, very often) taken to mean an entire group of rights, not a single right. For example, we say 'the right of external

ownership' when we mean 'the right of disposing of a given thing with complete freedom of will'. The second meaning includes an infinite number of actions and activities, each of which can be considered as a right.

There are, therefore, *complex and simple* rights. Complex rights include many simple rights. A simple right is an activity (whether potency or act, action or experience) that either cannot be further simplified in its real existence, or is understood as simple relative to other activities.

323. Obviously, the distinction between *simple* and *complex rights* is purely verbal and only explains the double use of the word 'right'. But the distinction is important for the order and logical clarity of the subject we are discussing. From it, we have this rule of method: 'To be certain that a right which has been made known to us exists in reality, we must first see whether it is complex. If it is, we must break it down and reduce it to simple rights. We must then demonstrate the existence of each of these.'

Failure to apply this rule can result in deception and the admission of non-existent rights. Very often we are satisfied that we have demonstrated a complex right in all its complexity, although our demonstration extends at most to only a majority of simple rights included in the complex right. As a result we mistakenly think we have fully demonstrated the existence of a total right. This explains the great number of errors and inexactitudes to be found in writers on the science of Right. It also explains our human propensity to false claims, and to constant litigation. However I do not think it necessary to use this rule of method all the time, because discussion would be prolonged excessively and sometimes uselessly. It is sufficient to have recourse to it whenever the uncertainty of the subject seems to demand it.

Article 2.
The distinction between what is *lawful* and what is *of right* — The second rule

324. Another source of errors in determining rights is the omission of anyone of the five characteristics of right. These

characteristics indicate a second rule of method for regulating the way we must derive and determine rights. It can be expressed as: 'The existence of a right is not rigorously demonstrated without the demonstration of the existence of each of its five constituents.'

Let us imagine that some simple activity is being carried on, as the preceding rule prescribed. In order to show that a right is present in this activity we must show that all five characteristics and constitutive elements of right are verified in the activity, namely, that it contains 1. physical activity, 2. personship, 3. eudaimonological value, 4. lawfulness, and 5. the duty in others to respect the activity.

325. This rule is clearly the source of the distinction between true rights and simply lawful actions . We cannot say we have a true right to do an action solely because it is lawful; we must always take account of the *jural duty* in others to leave us free. If this duty exists, the action acquires the nature of right. For example, an employer permits an employee to do many things which, relative to the employer, are not in the employee's right, simply because there is no jural duty in the employer to leave the other free; he could, if he wished, prohibit the other from acting.[181]

[181] Some systematic authors who recognise rights as coming only from the State or the government of civil society (things which they confuse) divide civil laws into *obligatory* and *permissive*. They maintain that *permissive laws* are the non-acts of a ruler, not those with which a ruler abrogates, modifies or suspends previously promulgated laws. A ruler, in their opinion, permits what he does not prohibit; the governative power extends its authority not only to all the things it positively intends, but tacitly to those things about which it says and disposes nothing. With this non-act it permits and ratifies! This is absurd; such a system favours not simply despotism but the greatest despotism, as I said earlier. It supposes that civil government is lord of all things and of all persons, and that nothing lies outside the limits of its authority. Anything it does not forbid, therefore, must be considered in the same light as the permission which an employer gives to his employee to use for himself the energy and time he has pledged to the employer!

Article 3.
The distinction between *complete* rights and rights *relative* to certain human beings — The third rule

326. It is therefore clear that the notion of right always involves a relationship (at least a possible relationship) with other human beings in whom a corresponding *jural duty* can be conceived. Hence rights are divided into *full* and *non-full* rights. The former are those which have a corresponding jural duty in all other human beings. The latter are rights relative not to all human beings but to those in whom there is a corresponding jural duty. In the latter case the action itself, which is a true right relative to those in whom the jural duty exists, is not a right relative to others who do not have the same jural duty. In this case the action will at most be a simply lawful action.

327. This observation has also been neglected, although it gives rise to a third rule of method for the discussion of rights. This rule can protect us from many errors. It states: 'If I have demonstrated that a moral duty to avoid impeding a given action does not exist in some human beings, I have not at the same time demonstrated that the action is not a true right relative to other human beings who have the moral duty to respect the action; I have simply demonstrated that the action is not a right relative to those individuals alone in whom the duty does not exist.' Thus, if an employee under obligation to his employer to work ten hours a day is granted a holiday for a fixed time, he acts licitly if he uses his time for his own advantage. Any action he now does licitly is not a right relative to his employer, who could always stop the holiday and recall him to work, but it can be considered a right relative to all other human beings who have the moral obligation not to deprive him of his freedom or the faculty of working for his own profit and pleasure.

Neglect of this distinction gave rise to innumerable useless, subtle and insoluble questions in the science of right. Is an action a right or not? Some authors, considering the action relative to one kind of persons, saw it as a right; others did not, because they considered it relative to other kinds of persons.

Article 4.
Other kinds of relative rights — he fourth rule

328. All the rights considered so far are contained in the true notion of right. But other rights exist which I have called *presumed rights.*[182] They are called rights because they must be considered and respected *as if they were rights*, although in themselves they are not. This kind must also be borne in mind if we are to avoid confusing them with true rights.

Such a distinction, which also constitutes a useful rule for solving many practical and scientific questions on right, provides the following important corollary: 'Although I must consider certain things in others as if they were true rights, I could never consider the same things as rights in myself.'

CHAPTER 2
The principle to be followed in the derivation and determination of rights

Article 1.
A false way of determining rights by means of the end to which they are ordered by nature

329. The majority of authors set out to derive and determine various rights in the human being from the end to which these rights are ordered by nature. For example, they say that there is an innate right to self-preservation because certain rights most certainly have as their end the conservation of human nature, that is, of the species. But this way of deriving rights from their ends is inexact and involves serious difficulties.

330. First, right as we have seen is 'an activity'. It seems more logical, therefore, to investigate the activities which constitute

[182] Cf. 292.

the subject of rights than to abandon the activities themselves in order to enquire about the end to which they tend.

Second, when I have determined a given end, for example, the preservation of my life, I have determined not a single right, but rather a complex of rights, composed of all the rights necessary for the preservation of my life. Nevertheless, I have still not truly proved that each action directed to preserve my life is a right that I have. I have to prove this before I can affirm it, as we have seen in establishing the first logical rule for the deduction of rights.[183]

Third, because it is certain that there are a number of unlawful things I can do to preserve my life (which as unlawful are not part of my right), it is equally certain that I cannot affirm my right to preserve my life in such a general manner. If I want to declare my right in this way, I have to qualify the declaration in order to determine its rightful limits. I must say: 'I have an innate right to preserve my life, but on condition that I employ only actions which fall within my right.' Such a formula is obviously pointless. If it is to be of any use, I have to state what these actions are to which I have a right, and with which, therefore, I can directly preserve my life. Such a vague right of preservation of life requires us to establish the activities which form the subjects of simple rights. Without knowing what these activities are, I cannot know what this vague right is. But if I know the activities which form subjects of my rights, it is clear that I can deduce as a corollary my right to all the good things which the use of these faculties brings in its wake. The preservation of my life is one of these good things, but only a special one amongst many.

331. It is clear, therefore, that rights cannot be deduced from their end, or from the good that they bring in their wake, but from the faculties and activities in which they exist. Nevertheless, we shall see that the consideration of the end of rights will be helpful and necessary after we have determined rights by means of the faculties and activities that constitute them. Consideration of the ends of activities will assist us in discovering what is changeable and what is unchangeable in these

[183] 322–323.

rights. This, in its turn, will lead us to the discovery of indefectible rights.

Article 2.
Ownership, as that which is proper to a person, is the general principle according which all rights are to be determined

332. So far we have determined rights by examining the good obtained through the exercise of rights (this good is sometimes immediate and sometimes mediate — another reason for its vagueness and imprecision). We can now leave this path and attempt to determine rights from the *activities* which are their subjects.

This determination will be totally clear, it seems to me, if we first look for the *general characteristic* indicating an activity in so far as this activity is subject of right relative to all rights in general, not solely to innate rights. When found, this characteristic will be sufficiently clear for us to note it in new-born babies and in adults at any stage whatsoever. As soon as we note it, we shall be in a position to know what rights, if any, a new-born person has, and what rights, if any, other people have in whatever state we care to consider them.

We shall indicate this characteristic with the single word OWNERSHIP the normal meaning of which we shall broaden, or rather refer the word back to its ancient, genuine meaning, in order to explain what we have in mind.

333. According to its original meaning, this word 'ownership' indicates the union of one thing (accident or substance) with another *individual* thing.[184] This conjunction is stable and complete, and brought about so exclusively that one thing is bound to another without being similarly bound to anything else. So, air and light are not said to be proper to any individual because

[184] According to Forcellini, the word *proprio* [in English, *proper*, *one's own*] seems to come from *prope*, 'near'. The same entry, when applied to words, is defined as follows by the great lexicographer: *Proprietas verborum, conjunctio illorum arcta et apta cum rebus ipsis quas significant* [What belongs to words in their strict and apt connection with the very things they signify]. Cf. under *Proprietas*.

they are not bound to any individual. They are common to all human beings because all can equally enjoy and use them, nor can anyone reach out for them and restrict them to his sole use.[185]

334. Analysing the general concept expressed by the word *ownership*, we find that it presupposes the co-existence of two things which can be mentally distinguished, and expresses a relationship between them. By this relationship one is bound to the other in such a way that it is owned by and serves the other totally and exclusively.

The same analysis shows us that because the word 'ownership' excludes what is *common*, that is, a share in the same thing by several individuals, the thing which holds the other as something which it *owns* must be an individual. The *owner* must be or must represent a single individual.

Moreover, the two things cannot be equal. Their relationship requires that the one bound and joined to the other be in an inferior condition to that to which it is united. The former has a relationship of dependence upon the latter; the latter has a relationship of independence from the other (if this can indeed be called a relationship). The thing which is owned by another does not exist except through its connection with the other, but that which owns can be thought of as existing by itself.

Two acts are found in the concept of one thing which owns another. The first act is its subsistence, independently of what it owns; the second is that with which it owns the other thing. That which owns supposes an existence in itself, not simply relative to other things.

335. Here we have to recall a teaching which seems to me necessary if a solid foundation is to be laid for right, although it does entail an effort of thought on the ontological level. Branches of knowledge are so intimately connected and truths are so linked that it is impossible for the human mind to be fully convinced of and satisfied by any derived truth unless it moves step by step to truths, or rather to the primitive truth. Only when the derived truth is seen in the primitive truth does the

185 'When he has bought from us all those things which we OWNED, 'he must not deprive us of the light which is held in COMMON' (Cicero, *Oratio pro Roscio Amerino*, 1: 2).

mind believe that it knows, and find rest in knowledge (as we have said from the beginning). I would ask permission, therefore, to recall now, and whenever the matter in hand requires it, ontological teaching, and connect it with the principle of the derivation of rights. The reader's own wisdom will see the necessity for this.

336. I have shown elsewhere that material things enjoy only an existence relative to feeling and intelligence.[186] Because they do not exist in THEMSELVES, it is clear that they cannot be owners of other things.

Nevertheless, we have to distinguish in material things an act of subsistence, which constitutes their specific essence,[187] from certain accidental acts intimately connected with their act of subsistence. This explains why everyday speech applies personal and possessive pronouns, *he*, *she*, *his, hers*, to things without feeling. We say: 'Let's consider the ship in *her*self. *She*'s grey. *Her* capacity is twenty thousand tons.' And we speak about *her* various *properties*. But these ways of speaking, and the concepts they express, are all subject to the 'transcendental critique of knowledge.'[188] It has been shown that not everything human beings believe they know corresponds to the truth and reality of things; even in our cognitions we ourselves posit a great deal as a result of the subjective laws of our spirit.

337. We are asking, therefore, if we ourselves gratuitously posit something in these concepts, in a way not in conformity with their absolute truth. And we find without difficulty that we bestow upon material things a mode of existence similar to that which we enjoy. From the beginning, there is no way by

186 Cf. *PE*, 21–47.

187 Cf. *OT*, 657–659.

188 By 'transcendental critique' I mean an examination of various *human cognitions* made through the highest and most evident principle of reason where, as we have seen, there cannot be error of any sort. The word 'transcendental' can, I think, be usefully conserved in philosophy provided that we understand it as including all that transcends the corporeal senses and all *materiated, relative cognitions*. But although 'a critique of human *cognitions*' can be carried out, it would be absurd to undertake a 'critique of reason.' Kant's mistake lies here: while it is possible for *reason* to criticise the special *cognitions* of human beings, it cannot criticise itself because it can never say of itself that it is wrong.

which we can see simply a relative existence in material things, that is, an existence which has nothing proper and absolute of its own. As a result, we change our own sensations, the effects of the force that modifies our feeling, into many different entities and individual things which we immediately furnish with some imaginary personship. We apply to them without difficulty pronouns indicating person or personal qualities, as if they effectively possessed both their own subsistence and personship.

It is true that there is a bond (something by way of principle and something accessory, something permanent and something changeable) in sensations, and in general in the effects produced in human feeling by material force. But the intrinsic order between these effects cannot constitute the bond of ownership. In the first place, such relationships have their origin principally in the constitution of the feeling subject itself, and cannot be referred to corporeal force. Secondly, even if they were to be carried over into the acting force itself, what is posited in the force would be nothing more than various powers of modifying the human feeling. These would indeed presuppose a subsistence, but a subsistence totally unknown to us in its own essence, and thus not forming part of the material object of which we have, or think we have, knowledge.[189]

We have to say, therefore, when speaking of the *ownership* of corporeal beings and applying to them *personal* or *possessive* pronouns, that the words we use have a true sense only if they are considered as metaphorical. If the concepts expressed by those words are to be rendered free of all false understanding they must be taken in a merely hypothetical sense in relationship to our mode of conceiving them mentally. In the same way, the subsistence of bodies is simply a subsistence dependent upon the laws of our mind and those of our feeling. This subsistence has nothing to render it personal, subjective, and proper to bodies as such.

338. These inanimate beings, therefore, have no existence of their own, and the word SELF is practically non-existent for

[189] Hence my distinction between *body* which we perceive and *corporeal principle* which we do not perceive. Cf. *OT*, 845.

them. They cannot be said to have anything *proper* to them. What is the situation for animate beings which lack reason?

Their existence is not merely objective, that is, relative simply to the one perceiving them, as in the case for beings without feeling. Feeling beings exist in a subjective mode. Nevertheless, it cannot be said of them that they *own* in the true sense of the word. We can prove this merely by considering what we have said: that is, *ownership* involves the concept of two things, the *owner* and that which he *owns*. The personal pronoun *himself* corresponds to the owner, and the possessive pronoun *his* to what he owns.[190] 'HIS thing' means the 'thing of HIM'. But I have already shown that the animal is only a substantial feeling.[191] And feeling is something unique which totally lacks SELF, MYSELF, I, which amount to the same thing. These words express an entirely *personal* principle, involving *consciousness* and therefore presupposing an intelligent principle capable of reflecting upon itself and seeing itself objectively. In a word, this subject objectivises itself by intuiting and perceiving the sentient principle as identified with the intelligent agent in the great mirror, as we may call it, of being in general. The *personal* principle, therefore, is the principle of *ownership*; SELF is the principle of what is PROPER TO ONESELF, of what is owned by self. 'Self' must exist before 'his' can exist. But 'self' cannot exist except in an intellective being. Consequently, there can be no true *ownership*, nothing that is *proper to oneself*, owned by oneself, except in an intellective being.

339. Jurists use the word 'ownershiip' exactly, therefore, when they employ it to express 'the dominion that a person has over something.' This is ownership in the genuine meaning of the word which truly expresses 'the strict union of a *thing* with a *person* by means of which that thing is reserved totally and exclusively to the person as if it were part of him.' *Mine* does in

[190] Consequently, the word 'own', 'proper', is perhaps used in all languages to replace the possessive pronouns *his*, *yours*, *mine*. For example, amongst Latin authors, Livy uses : *Non placebat Socios* propriis viribus *consiliisque bella gerere* [The allies were not happy about waging war on the basis of their own strength and advice] (bk 2, c. 53) instead of *suis viribus* [on the basis of their strength].

[191] Cf. *AMS*, bk 2.

fact express a part of 'self', something that belongs to 'self'. But in this intimate connection, SELF, the person, does not and cannot lose personal dignity. Consequently, the thing is inherent to the person of whom it forms a subjective, accessory part, dominated by SELF, which, as the personal principle, does what it wishes with what is ITS OWN, precisely because it is the person's own and is proper to him. This kind of union, which is called *ownership*, always occurs between a person and a thing, and includes *dominion* by the former over the latter.

Article 3.
Continuation. — Jural freedom

340. We call this dominion of the person over what is connected to him and forms one thing with him 'jural freedom', as soon as it is considered as a principle of *activity* and source of actions. It is clear that here the word 'freedom' takes on a rather different meaning from that given it in the phrase 'bilateral freedom', which indicates a special manner of action on the part of the will.[192] *Jural freedom* means only 'that relationship of governance that a owner has towards what he owns, enabling him morally to use it as he wishes.'

It could happen that some kind of morally obligatory law impedes or limits the use that a person can make of something that is his own. In this case, the law would limit not only the *jural freedom* of the person, but even his right of *ownership*. *His* ownership of what is proper would be reduced to the extent that the obligatory law prevented him from using it as he wishes. As we can see, the idea of *ownership* essentially embraces and contains that of *freedom* (of free use). *Ownership*, therefore, is normally defined as 'the faculty of disposing as one pleases, without interference from others, of the substance of a thing, and of what is useful in it.'[193]

However, we shall have to speak later about *jural freedom* considered as an attribute of the *ownership* which we are examining. We shall take the opportunity of doing this when we

[192] Cf. *AMS*, 606–611.

[193] Cf. the Austrian Civil Code, §354.

examine the modes which, extending or limiting this *freedom*, are consequently related to *ownership*.

Article 4.
Continuation

341. For the moment, we have to recall what we said at the beginning: we do not limit the meaning of the word *ownership* to dominion over external things. We take it in its original, natural significance which involves all that a person has joined to himself as part of himself, that is, as *his*. In this meaning, as we said, the word *ownership* is highly appropriate in indicating the *characteristic* differentiating the existence of rights and jural duties. Accordingly, ownership constitutes a *sphere* around the person in which the person is the *centre*. No one else can enter this sphere, and no one can separate from the person that which is inherent in him as a result of the connection between him and what is his own. This kind of separation would cause *suffering* to the person. But suffering (considered in itself), when imposed upon a person, is forbidden as evil by the moral law.

Article 5.
Comparison of the principle proposed by us for the determination of rights with the principle of possible co-existence followed almost universally in Germany

342. The principle we have adopted for the derivation and determination of rights is composed of two elements, one of which is a *fact*. This is the sphere, called 'ownership' or 'sphere of ownership', around the person. The other is something commanded by the moral law which states: 'Do no harm to persons by separating any part of themselves from themselves, that is, any part contained within the sphere of their ownership.'

We must now compare this simple, universal principle with the principle of *possible co-existence* proposed by Kant and then embraced, with impressive assent, by practically the whole of Germany and by the legislations adopted in that learned country. This is how Zeiller, a noteworthy author, sets out the principle in his *Diritto privato naturale*:

> A human being existing amongst others of his species is made aware by his own feeling that he can avoid self-contradiction only by refraining from treating his fellows as simple means to his own ends and by undertaking to accept them as other *persons*. When he has to carry out some external actions which could affect his fellows he cannot therefore lay claim to unlimited freedom, but must of his own accord impose on himself the limits necessary to avoid the contradiction we have mentioned. In other words, human beings can be considered solely according to their essence, as they are in this case, only as a result of equal limitation on the part of all. Restriction on the freedom of each human being, established in such a way that all can exist equally as *persons*, constitutes *right* taken in its absolute sense, as we know from our own feeling.[194]

A careful analysis of this way of determining rights shows: 1. that it does not necessarily include a moral limitation of one's own physical activity; 2. that even if it did, the limitation would not be a complete, moral limitation; 3. that it is sufficient to determine some rights, but not all; finally, 4. that it lacks necessary precision because it does not determine how much limitation each human being has to impose on the exercise of his own natural activity. We now have to consider each of these four deficiencies in detail.

§1. *The first deficiency in the principle which determines rights by means of the possibility of co-existence of persons: this principle does not necessarily include the characteristic, 'morality'*

343. The explanation of the Kantian principle of the determination of rights states, in part: 'A human being is made aware by his *own* feeling that he cannot avoid self-contradiction unless he undertakes to accept others of his species as *persons*.' But are we speaking here of a truly moral duty, or rather of a simple, logical

[194] Introduction, §3.

rule which, if contradicted, would render a human being in contradiction with himself? Or are we speaking of a rule of prudence by which a human being sees that his neglect to limit the use of his faculties would cause others to do the same with consequent loss of his entire freedom? In the final case, he would justly conclude that it would be better for him to sacrifice one part willingly to the greater force of others than to lose another. If we are dealing with a simple *rule of logic* teaching us to avoid contradiction, or with a *mere rule of prudence* founded in self-interest (not in true respect for others), there would indeed be no genuine limitation and determination of right because such limitation can only be moral.

In fact, it seems that *prudence* has been substituted for *morality* in the spirit of this principle, if we consider that the force of the argument is founded entirely on the co-existence of persons and can therefore be expressed in the following form: 'It is necessary for persons to co-exist. But they can co-exist only if each of them limits himself in the exercise of his own freedom. It is therefore necessary for each of them to limit himself.' The whole force of the argument is found in the major proposition, that is, in the supposition that 'the co-existence of persons is necessary'. But we could ask why the co-existence of persons is *necessary*. Are we speaking about moral necessity, or some necessity arising from the interest each human being has in his own existence? The explanation of the principle which we have examined provides no answer. But if the necessity of co-existence is indeed to be understood as the interest each person has in preserving his own personal existence (which would mean preserving part of his own activity by sacrificing another part to others), we depend totally upon a calculation of prudence. The moral element has disappeared. Our presupposition does not give rise to a state of right, but to a state of fact, useful to all.[195]

[195] Such a state of fact useful to all could not be sustained for long without some moral sanction. It is impossible for individuals, guided by principles of self-interest, to persuade themselves that their own personal interest would always gain some advantage from the respect shown to the personal interest of others. Nor would those in more favourable circumstances be restrained from profiting at the expense of others. Cf. my comments on the subject in

§2. *The second deficiency: the principle would not be complete even if it included the characteristic of morality*

344. Let us grant that the proposition is concerned with *moral necessity* and can be expressed as follows: 'Each person has the moral duty to provide for his own and others' personal preservation, and has therefore the duty to restrict the use of his own activity, etc.' This is undoubtedly a moral limit, but it is not based on a sufficient reason, or at least has no sufficient, expressed reason. The manner in which each person must restrict his freedom is still not manifest.

345. In fact, a difficulty presents itself immediately to the spirit: if each individual has to limit himself in the exercise of his own freedom by virtue of a special moral obligation (the obligation arising from the co-existence of persons), why is this limitation not influenced by any other obligation decreed by the principle of ethics? Again: is there no moral obligation other than that which makes personal co-existence possible between ourselves and our fellows? An answer to this difficulty could be made along the following lines: 'Yes, there are other ethical laws which impose limits in the use of our faculties, but they do not determine natural right.'

However, the difficulty could be pressed by insisting that natural right cannot be taught scientifically unless some reason (not gratuitous assertions) is provided for the affirmation. The proponent now finds himself forced to maintain that people have the right to use their own faculties, but that such a right when extended universally will either unleash war (if the faculties are exercised limitlessly), or require limitation in the use of the faculties (in such a way that each person retains freely and safely the greatest possible *equal* portion of that right). Despite the excellence of the reply, we still have to insist: 1. the right under consideration is not explained, but presupposed as innate in each person — only the limitation of the right is explained; 2. it is false, therefore, that the limitation, that is, the obligation that each has to limit the exercise of his own freedom, formally constitutes the right.

Opuscoli Filosofici, vol 2, p. 387 ss.

Summing up, we may say that either we admit an innate right to an unlimited use of our own faculties[196] or grant that such unlimited use, before it is restricted by duty, is simply a physical fact unrelated to morality and foreign to right. In the first case, the moral duty of restricting the use of the right does not form, but presupposes the right; in the second case, we have to admit that the physical fact must receive all the limitation imposed on it by moral legislation, as we have said.[197] We are not dealing with a single precept of moral legislation, that is, with the obligation to leave others the possibility of existing as persons. The freedom to act which results from fulfilling this single precept is still not a truly moral freedom if at the same time it offends other equally moral precepts. In this case, it is simply physical freedom arbitrarily limited.

[196] This is a repetition of Spinoza's error. He was attracted by the word 'nature', which he interpreted as the opposite of *reason*, or even as the opposite of *positive law*. If *reason* is withdrawn from *nature*, only *physical activity* remains. This physical activity cannot, however, be called 'right'. The system of right adopted by Spinoza is false precisely because of this abuse of the word 'nature'. Roman laws were guilty of the same kind of abuse in applying the word 'right' even to beasts. Hobbes, who also took 'nature' in this sense, virtually denied the existence of a right of nature. According to him: 'The effect of its right' (his pretended right of nature) 'is almost the same as if there were no right at all. Although each person could say: "This is my right", no one could enjoy the right because of the presence of his neighbour who would claim an equal right and equal force as his own. — Therefore justice towards human beings presupposes human laws which in the state of nature are non-existent' (*De Civ.*, c. 1, §102 ss.). Hobbes' error consists in his inability to see any limit to physical force other than human laws. The difference between Hobbes and Kant, therefore, is that Hobbes requires the *civil law*, upheld by force, as the limiting factor of natural activity; Kant finds the limiting factor in the *law of reason* which itself has to be converted into civil law and maintained by force on the part of the State. The difference between the two views is immense, but it does not prevent our seeing how Kant arrived at his own system through studying and meditating Hobbes' book and the works of Spinoza.

[197] Elsewhere we have distinguished a kind of lawfulness or moral freedom (which is relative to special legislations) from lawfulness or absolute moral freedom (which is relative to moral legislation taken in all its extension).

§3. *The third deficiency: the principle can determine some rights, but not all*

346. Kant's principle of the determination of rights, as developed by Zeiller, offers another great difficulty. It is founded upon an *abstraction*, which does not exist in nature but is only a part of what exists in nature. In other words, it requires us to consider human beings according to their essence, without reference to their accidental differences.

If it were true that people living on earth possessed only the essence of human nature, without any accidental additions, this principle might be useful in deducing the rights existing between living, human essences. But it is not true. In fact, we possess infinite particulars that do not form part of our human essence but which, nevertheless, serve as the basis of varying relationships between us, and of varying rights. In other words, the principle in question, when it considers us as naked essences devoid of all particulars, could at most lead us to hypothetical, abstract rights, but not to true, real rights that bind people together. And it is these rights for which we are searching.

347. This abstract principle, which presupposes that all human beings are equal (that is, possess human essence, but nothing more), does in fact assign to each an equal share of freedom or free action. But it is precisely this arithmetically equal quantity of free action which is never verified in reality. People are naturally unequal as a result of their inborn talents, powers, and so on, and as a consequence of their varying age, etc. It is completely impossible, therefore, for them all to exercise the same share of activity, and sacrifice the same share to the co-existence of others. Many would not have even that amount of activity, even considered as a whole, which would be present in the single portion sacrificed by other individuals. In this case, something approaching an equal portion could be preserved for each individual only if the members of the first group kept all that they had, and the second group sacrificed, say, more than half of what they possessed; and something approaching an equal portion could be sacrificed only if the first group sacrificed all they had, and the second not even a half. In other words, it is impossible to unite these two things in such a way that an

equal quantity is kept by all, and an equal quantity sacrificed by all.

348. In the theory under consideration we have to understand 'share' taken proportionately, not arithmetically and absolutely, as the portion to be sacrificed or kept by each person. Otherwise, the principle would have no possible meaning. But if the principle is understood as we have stated, its whole basis is overthrown; people are considered as furnished with their natural inequalities, and are not taken more precisely as though furnished solely with human essence.

349. I am aware that authors begin by abstracting human nature in order to determine natural rights amongst human beings, and that they glory in this defect of their system rather than acknowledge it. They are persuaded of the perfection of their method because, as they say, they have ascended to what is universal and to the sphere of pure reason.[198] But it should be easy to convince them of the ineptitude of this method by showing that they unconsciously abandon it in their works and thus themselves demonstrate that the method cannot be followed coherently, and that even if this were possible, it would not be very helpful.

No author on rational Right has ever maintained from start to finish the abstraction of human nature on which, according to him, he has founded the science of right. No author has ever laid down a law for himself which required him to speak constantly of perfect human equality, and therefore of equal relationships between human beings, without referring to any accidental difference of state or circumstances. If he had, and had kept to his proposal, he would have experienced no difficulty in finishing his work in record time. But let us take one example to show what we mean.

All these authors deal with contracts in which the two persons concerned are always in different and opposite relationship by

[198] Zeiller grants that the notion of right which he gives is rather different from that in normal use, but this is a recommendation in his eyes: 'The scientific meaning of right varies from that embraced by common usage in this respect alone: the former indicates the essential notes of the object with the greatest possible abstraction — and this is as it should be' (§2 of his *Diritto privato naturale*).

the very fact that they are making a contract. If they are buying and selling, one possesses what the other has not got, but wants to acquire. These are two accidents of human nature which do not belong to the essence of the human being, but place the contracting partners in different, opposite states relative to right.

In the same way, the authors speak about natural associations, for example, the domestic association. But in such an association, husband, wife and children are not considered as though they possessed human nature and nothing more. They are people endowed with accidents and inequalities, and their rights cannot be deduced simply by starting from the principle (desired by these authors) that 'each of these three members should respect the co-existence of the other two, and that each should sacrifice an equal share of his own freedom and retain an equal share (but no more) of the exercise of freedom.' The special rights of husband, wife and child would never be found on the basis of such a principle which, therefore, is useless and sterile, and can never serve as the starting point of a complete treatment of natural right. As we said, it can be employed at most in an imperfect treatise, which will be confined to a hypothetical, abstract, partial and not very useful teaching on the subject.

350. I am also aware how this abstraction of human nature proves attractive enough to be considered as a suitable foundation for natural right.

First, *personship* found in human *nature* lends weight to that principle. I myelf take the dignity of person, or rather the element which gives person its dignity, as the universal reason for rights and, prior to that, even as the source of duties. But while it is just to take the person as the *universal reason for rights*, it is unjust and false to claim that person alone is the *principle of the derivation or determination of rights*. Note, too, that the human person is not human nature, but only an element in this nature.[199]

351. I am sure that my readers will find it helpful here if I show the immense difference between the following two questions:

[199] Cf. *AMS*, bk 4.

'What is the title or universal reason for rights (in scholastic language, the *formal principle*)?' and: 'What is the principle of the determination of rights?' The 'principle of the determination of rights' is not quite what others call the 'material principle' (*principum materiale*) if this is taken to mean the principle which assigns to rights their matter. It is rather a middle principle between the *formal* and the *material* principle. In other words, it is a principle which teaches and directs the mind to link the form and the matter of rights and thus to enunciate and determine rights themselves.

352. The principle of co-existence amongst human beings, which we are at present examining and find insufficient for its purposes, claims to be such a principle. It does indeed contain the formal principle, personship, which is only an element, although the most important element, of human nature. But it does not lead us to unite the formal principle with the entire matter of rights. It confines us to that part of the matter which is found in human nature considered abstractly. As a result, the formal principle itself 1. cannot be accepted as an altogether pure and simply formal principle because it expresses not only human personship, but abstract human nature in which are found, along with personship, other elements which are the matter, not the form, of right; 2. nor can it be accepted even as a 'principle of determination' because it does not determine all the matter of rights, but only that part included in human nature. It does not extend to the part made up of the accidents, modifications, developments and acquired relationships of this nature.

353. Moreover, the universality of the principle 'of the possibility of co-existence' proved illusory to those embracing it because of the abstraction to which it was raised. It is true, of course, that none of us hopes for universality now, or seeks it. But there is universality and universality: abstract and one-sided universality which consists in drawing together simply the common characteristics of things; and universality which, in addition to the common characteristics, embraces the individual characteristics and the things themselves. This complete universality extends to everything required by and included in the argument under discussion.

The *onesidedness* of the first kind of universality can be seen as soon as we realise that it includes only common, not individual characteristics nor the things themselves contained in the class of which we are speaking. The *totality* of the second kind of universality is seen as soon as we realise that it omits nothing, and embraces all that is required, that is, everything which forms the matter of the discussion.

354. It is clear that scientific propositions must be furnished with the kind of universality required by the aim of the discussion, that is, by the object of the branch of knowledge. If this object is abstract, its propositions must be characterised by the first kind of universality. If such propositions were not abstract, they would be defective because more inclusive than the theme of the branch of knowledge itself.

Purifying these propositions of all superfluity is the work of the learned. Teachings, which are in human minds long before they are put into scientific form, take on the dignity of ordered knowledge when they are distributed in propositions which rigorously express nothing more than is needed for the object or theme of the particular branch of knowledge. Everything else is rejected as superfluous, as chaff mixed with the pure gold of intellectual work after the other powers have carried out their operations contemporaneously.

We must note carefully, however, that we can run into the opposite error when, by separating and purifying common propositions, we remove their superfluities. As we eliminate heterogeneous matters by separating out what is foreign to the argument, we may also remove part of the argument itself. And this accounts for errors in teachings which are excessively abstract. Authors want to put these teachings into ever more scientific form, but often make them more abstract than necessary. The result is to deprive them of parts that are indeed the aim of the science that these writers wish to elucidate.

When the object of the science under discussion is not abstract, however, it must surely be clear that the propositions composing the branch of knowledge must be characterised by the second kind of universality, not the first. Abstract propositions would never express the object of the science, and consequently never be adequate for the theme.

355. Summing up, we may say that 'propositions, in order to be scientific, must always be universal, but not always be abstract. They have to include all that the theme of the science

demands, and exclude all that it does not demand.' All that *the theme of the science* demands shows the degree of *universality* that these propositions must have; *all that the theme of the science does not demand* shows the degree of abstraction that the propositions must also have, neither more nor less.

In our view, the principle 'of the possibility of co-existence' has too low a degree of *universality*, and too high a degree of *abstraction*. The degree of *universality* is too low because it does not include all that is required by the theme of the science; it embraces only abstract human nature, though the largest part of rights between human beings has its special title in the accidents of human nature. The degree of *abstraction* is too high because the theme of the science of natural Right does not exclude the accidents of human nature if these depend upon natural laws and (here we take natural Right in a stricter sense than usual) if they are not dependent upon agreements, or at least on the state of civil society.

Our principle of *ownership* (in the sense we give to this word), may be compared from this point of view with that of *co-existence*. The former is obviously as *universal* as it should be. It can be used to determine all human rights, as we shall see when we come to apply it and understand that the characteristic of *ownership* is found whenever right is present. At the same time, the proposition is not more *abstract* than it should be. *Ownership* is formed by means of accidents also, which play their part in human nature.

§4. *Fourth deficiency: the principle does not determine the quantity of limitation that each individual must impose on the exercise of his own activity*

356. Finally, the principle 'of the possibility of co-existence' would be of little advantage in the derivation of rights. Although it requires from each person the limitation of his own activity in such a way that the use of the same activity is open to other people (which is impossible, as we have seen),[200] no principle is

[200] Cf. 346–352.

available with which to judge in practice the precise quantity of limitation. It is too vague to maintain that limitation should be sufficient to enable others to co-exist as persons. This means that it cannot have any precise, universal outcome, as we can see more easily from the following reflections.

357. It certainly cannot be affirmed that the presence of another human being as a person along with me depends upon the *quantity* of limitation that I impose on my own freedom, nor that my existence as a person depends upon the limitation placed by another individual upon his own activity. By personal existence we mean that portion of activity which remains at my free disposition without being comprised in the limitation I impose upon myself in order not to block equal activity in others. My self-imposed limitation, whatever its quantity, does not eliminate my existence and operation as a person. In fact, by imposing it upon myself I carry out the personal activity of auto-limitation. The same must be said in regard to any other person: limitation, when willed, never eliminates anyone's existence as a person because it does not take away from the use of one's own free will, in which consists the personal element.

It may be objected that we are not dealing here with self-imposed limitation, but with the limitation that one person imposes upon another; it is precisely this which can take away people's personal existence. But how is this proved? If one person limits another, the imposed limitation is either received willingly, whatever its quantity, or it has no effect. If it is received willingly, it cannot be an obstacle to the personal existence of the persons in whom it is received. As we have said, when the imposition is received willingly it does not diminish the exercise of personal activity but posits it. If it is not received willingly, we may indeed grant that it limits and impedes personal existence and operation in some way. But we can only infer from this the general truth that however large or small the limitation used by one individual on another, the personal existence of the second is never rendered impossible. With his free will, he can always will that limitation for himself in such a way that it is no longer an obstacle to his personal existence, except in the special case of the destruction of his life. The possibility of the co-existence of human beings as persons does not necessarily depend, therefore, on the precise *quantity* of limitation that each individual imposes upon his own operations. It depends rather upon the disposition of his own will which may be more or less resigned, more or less strong, more or less virtuous.

The objection may be pressed again, but rather forcefully this time. According to my adversaries, what I have said indicates a complete misunderstanding of the principle of co-existence which I am refuting. They agree that the limitation imposed upon an individual by himself, or willingly received from others, does not impede personal existence or operation. But, they say, no one will willingly accept a limitation imposed upon him by another if he sees that such a limitation is unjust. And even if he were virtuous enough to bear such a gracious sacrifice for the sake of others, would he be obliged to do so? The principle of the possibility of co-existence only means, therefore, that human beings who live together must each limit their activity in such a way that if their operation limits that of another, the limitation or obstacle placed on the other's activity should not be greater than the limitation they each place on themselves. In other words, auto-limitation and the limitation imposed upon others should be *equal*. In the light of this equality, others have to accept the limitation willingly. Thus, it does not impede their personal existence and operation. This explanation does not, however, assist in ameliorating the principle of co-existence.

358. First, I note that such a principle would give each one the right to limit others with his own activity as much as he limits himself. Now I do understand that an individual can limit his own activity as much as he wants, but I cannot understand how the limit he imposes upon himself gives him the right to limit others in the same way. It is indeed lawful for each to limit himself as much as he wishes, but it does not follow from this that it is lawful to limit others beyond a certain point.

This reflection is sufficient for us to conclude that even when the limitation I place on others is entirely equal to that which I place upon my own activity, such equality does not render the quantity of limitation just, nor originate in others the obligation of willingly accepting it. The *equality* of the limitation imposed upon myself and others does not render *just* the quantity of limitation that I impose upon others with my activity. This *justice*, this just quantity of limitation which I may lawfully impose on others, must therefore be sought elsewhere. It cannot result from the characteristic of equality. Hence the principle of co-existence neither 1. reveals the precise *quantity* of limitation that each has to impose upon himself and is able to impose upon others; nor 2. includes the *reason* proving that the said quantity of limitation imposed upon others conforms to justice.

359. On the other hand, none of these objections can be applied to the principle of the determination of rights which I have proposed, that is: 'Respect that which belongs to others.' In this principle:

1. The *quantity of free activity* that each one can keep is assigned. It consists of all that can be exercised without harming the *ownership* of others.

2. In the same way, the *quantity of limitation* that each one must impose on his own operations is assigned. This limitation is not formed by his own calculation, according to which he decides the point at which unimpeded activity is limited by the personal co-existence of others. Such a calculation is impossible and without foundation. What matters is the positive *fact* of others' ownership, which varies, and in its variation limits his own activity accordingly, but always justly.

3. A clear *reason* is given for the justice of the *quantity* of limitation that each one has to impose upon himself. This reason is to be found in the universal, ethical command obliging us not to harm others. Damaging what belongs to others means imposing some harm upon them. Each person's activity, therefore, discovers an unsurpassable, moral limit, in others' ownership.[201]

[201] Many other comments could be made on the principle 'of the possibility of co-existence'. Some were explained in my *Storia comparativa e critica de' sistemi morali*, c. 5, art. 11.

CHAPTER 3

The principle determining the harm done to rights

360. If the principle of the determination of rights is true, it must contain in itself the principle determining the harm done to rights themselves. But the principle of *ownership* which we have proposed offers us the possibility of showing the extent and the quantity of damage done to rights. In fact, when each human being's sphere of ownership is sufficiently known, 'damage will be done every time that another individual departs from his own sphere and enters another's. The amount of the damage will depend upon the extent to which one has entered the other's sphere.'

Only the formal right of personal freedom is exempt from this principle because this right receives its determination in a negative manner alone, through the exclusion of ownership exterior to the person. Hence, damage to this right consists solely in an *attempt* made to harm the pure freedom of the human person. But all this will receive greater light from what we propose to say in the treatise of derived Right, where we shall explain the more special characteristics of ownership, and outline its sphere.

Appendix

1. (242).

It is curious to see how Roman laws brought beasts within the ambit of natural right, while denying *personship*, and consequently the capacity for right, to human beings themselves, such as slaves. These two extreme errors would alone be sufficient to moderate the exaggerated opinion of the wisdom of Roman laws which is still prevalent amongst certain people. Such wisdom can be admired only when it is compared with the state of the pagan world; it vanishes when brought face to face with Christianity. Our codes of law acknowledge all human beings as persons without distinction. Consider the noble words found in the Austrian code: 'Every human being has innate rights which can be known through reason alone. Each human being is, therefore, to be considered as a person' (§16). These words, which emphasise human dignity, are the result of Christianity. The principle behind them is already found in Justinian's *Institutes* (bk. 1, tit. 8) where the title 'person' begins to be used of slaves in whom indefectible rights are recognised and defended.

Relative to the first error, several ancient philosophers realised how false it was to institute a natural right common to beasts. Cicero, following Chrysippus, considers that rights cannot be rendered common to beasts: 'And as they understand that the obligations of right exist amongst human beings and between human beings, so they realise that there is no right common to human beings and beasts' (bk. 3, *De Finib.*, 20). But Roman laws are mutually contradictory when on one hand they grant right to beasts, and on the other derive the word *jus* from *justitia* while going on to define justice as 'a constant and perpetual will of attributing to each his right' (*Instit.*, 1: 15), a definition accepted by Cicero himself (*De Finib.*, 5: 23. Cf. also Plutarch's *Cato*). There is no doubt that beasts are without such a will simply because they have no will at all. Hence Cicero says: 'Nor are we further from the nature of beasts than in this matter. We do, indeed, often predicate fortitude, say, of horses or lions, but we never speak of their justice, or equity, or goodness because they are totally without reason and speech' (*De Offic*., 1: 16). Cicero does, however, confuse physical force with the virtue of fortitude.

The error which permits natural right as something common to human beings and beasts springs from granting too much to *sensuality*; the error which denies all right to slaves comes from granting too much to *sociality*. In pagan times, society was no less a tyrant than individuals. Society was egoistic. Individual subjects attributed everything to themselves; and civil society, composed of individuals, also attributed everything to itself. Human nature, objectively considered, counted for nothing; absolutism and tyranny were everywhere unassailable necessities.

The gradual descent by which human minds came to the solemn formulation of such nonsense (a *right of nature* common to beasts!) would provide material for lengthy, careful consideration. The very ancient use of *jus*, *justum*, for '*equal*', '*on a par with*', could have been an element in the decline. In fact, the primitive meaning of the word has no moral or intelligent significance. It simply expresses equality or conformity between one thing and another, between one quantity and another, and hence between animal acts and animal instincts. Another step towards this error is pointed out in chapter 4.

2. (289).

I refer obligation to *duty* rather than to the *moral law* in order to avoid the problem about permissive laws which has been taken up recently by Hübner against Burlamachi who sustains the laws of simple permission. However, an observation on the discussion will not be out of place.

The difference of opinions about the question, 'Do only permissive laws exist?' (cf. Suarez, *De Legib*., bk 1, c. 14–17), arose because one side was thinking of *natural law*, and the other side of *positive law*. The expression, 'merely permissive moral law', in itself implies a contradiction, if 'permitted action' means 'lawful action'. An action is rendered morally lawful by the *absence* of a prohibitive law. Natural law permits nothing, but commands everything; what is not commanded is permitted and lawfully carried out. — But this is not the case when we are speaking about *positive laws* to which belong the four principal effects of law enumerated by the lawyer Modestino: 'The power of law lies in commanding, prohibiting, permitting, punishing' (in bk. 7 of *De Legib.*). Positive law is able to *permit* because it can *prohibit* things not prohibited by natural law. Even when the legislator has *prohibited* such things, he can with a new law *permit* them by abrogating or limiting the prohibitive law. The word 'permit' properly speaking expresses a positive act of law. Hence anyone insisting on the propriety of the word could simply maintain that *permitting* is always done through a law; without a law, the action would certainly be *lawful* but could not be called *permitted*. In any case, a positive *permissive* law would properly speaking be a suspension or total or partial destruction of a previous positive law and nothing more than a negation clothed in external, positive forms of law.

Furthermore it is most important to maintain the distinction between what is simply *lawful* and what is positively *permitted*. Neglect of this distinction has produced a system of Right favourable to despotism in civil laws. The following argument is used to pass from such imprecision to despotism: '*Lawful* and *permissive* are the same. But nothing is permitted except what is permitted by the laws of the State, because *to permit* is an act of law. Therefore everything that is *lawful* is lawful in virtue of the civil laws which permit it.' This is deplorable sophistry. The truth is that there is an immense difference between something *not prohibited* by civil laws, something *permitted* by civil laws, and something *lawful*. Something *not prohibited* by civil laws is that over which these laws exercise no act, not even a permissive act. However, the thing is not always *lawful*; it can be prohibited by natural law, even in the absence of a positive law forbidding it. Something *permitted* by civil laws is either prohibited by a previous law or, because it is uncertain, is *permitted* by a new law, or declared free. Positive law exercises a negative act towards this thing by removing either the prohibition that previously regulated the action or the doubt about it. Even an action expressly *permitted* by positive laws is not necessarily *lawful*; it can be contrary to natural law. A *lawful* action therefore is simply an action which is not prohibited either by natural law, or any other obligatory law.

3. (316).

Those responsible for Roman right knew that its source and substance lay entirely in the moral law, and that *right* sprang from *duty.* Consequently, they posited moral precepts as the foundation of laws. Justinian's *Institutes* proclaimed: 'The precepts commanded by right are these: to live uprightly, not to harm others, and to grant each one his due' (bk. 1, *De just. et jure*, tit. 1). — However, these great men had not seen the difference between *moral duties, considered without qualification*, and *jural-moral duties*. This is clear from the precepts we have indicated. They extend further than jural-moral duties, but are nevertheless called *precepts commanded by right*. This lack of careful advertence to the limits of jural-moral duty was the cause of many errors, especially in the description of the sphere of positive legislation. The extension of jurisprudence was defined as follows: 'Jurisprudence is the knowledge of divine and human affairs, the science of what is just and what is unjust' (*Ibid.*) This led jurists to think they could abrogate to themselves the title of priests and take on the mission of declaring in all cases what was licit and what was not. 'Right is the art of what is good and what is equitable. Because of this we are called priests. We cultivate justice, we unfold the knowledge of what is good and what is equitable by separating what is equitable from what is evil, and discerning what is lawful and what is unlawful. We desire to make people good not only by fear of punishment, but also by holding out rewards; and unless I am mistaken, we practise true, not lying philosophy' (bk. 1 ss., *De justitia et jure*).

The quotation shows how morality is reduced totally to external laws; and how an attempt is made, by means of social laws alone, to judge what is good and equitable, and to distinguish what is just from what is unjust, what is lawful from what is unlawful. We should ponder, too, the claim these great jurists make of professing true, not lying philosophy. They realised that the commands of moral philosophy were spineless, and thought that public laws, furnished with punishments and rewards, would be more effective than the simple words of philosophers in inducing men and women to practise moral goodness. But human nature needs quite different means from these. Rome fell as her marvellous legislation grew more and more perfect. The inefficacy of *laws* in reforming human behaviour is examined in my *Society and its Purpose*, bk. 3, cc. 9–13.

But even if civil laws with their punishments and rewards were capable of influencing the human heart (which they are not), they would still enfold only a part of moral legislation, not the whole of moral teaching. We should remember:

1. Social laws can forbid evil, but are unable to command beneficence, which forms the best part of morality.

2. Social laws cannot even forbid the whole of evil, but only the part which constitutes an injury to jural duty.

3. Social laws have a third limitation: they can inflict punishment not on all the injuries done to jural duty, but only on the harm shown in provable material acts, which fall under the senses. As long as the harm is merely internal and unproven, it cannot be punished. At the same time, there could be many unprovable, external injuries, while the spirit itself could contain a jural injury through a deliberate will and decree to offend another person in his rights. Consequently, social laws, which can focus only on the external, material part of jural injury, and not on the moral part which is always hidden, have to judge the existence of internal harm from the existence of external damage. Such a judgment is not always infallible.

4. A fourth limitation springs from the necessity of expressing civil laws in words. As a result of this necessity, civil laws can never focus upon, determine and set out in a graded fashion all the external, material injuries of jural duty, not only because many elude the legislator's foresight, but also because 1. if they were all expressed in words, the quantity of legislation would make its use difficult, if not impossible; 2. language itself, as an imperfect instrument, would not be able to express matters with complete clarity.

5. Finally, the fifth limitation of social laws consists in their

procedure and the immense difficulties encountered in applying them when an *injury* has to be proved with certainty, as it must be. Very often this cannot be done; many injuries remain therefore outside the sanction of civil laws. And where injury is proved, the proof is not obtained with infallible certainty. On the other hand, an injury is sometimes thought to be proved when no injury existed.

It is indeed extraordinary that so many limitations which restrict the sphere of morality embraced by social laws should have been overlooked by the great men of old. Moreover, they very often went on to confuse *morals* with *civil law*, to which they reduced all human duties! Plato himself shows in many places that he held this opinion, and Aristotle speaks of the public laws as though they were a lesson in perfect virtue! These authorities, and the imperfect idea of moral goodness prevalent at their time, were the object of Cicero's own exaggerated eulogy of civil laws: 'From these (laws), we see how honour is to be sought in the best way: just and upright labour is rewarded with honours, rewards and splendour; human vice and deceit suffer punishment, shame, chains, stripes, exile and death. We are taught not by interminable arguments full of sophistries, but by the authority and fear of the laws, to control our lust, to hold our longings in check, to safeguard what is ours, and to withhold our minds, eyes and hands from what belongs to others' (*De Orat*. 1: 43).

All this shows clearly that moral teaching was far from being known in all its fullness before the coming of Jesus Christ. And the contemporary idea that public laws could fashion upright people is easily explained if we remember that legal uprightness and immunity from great crimes must have appeared extraordinary, and wonderful holiness. What is truly difficult to grasp is the way in which this error, which reduces moral goodness to keeping the civil laws, has been propagated right up to the present day. We often find jurists maintaining that it is they who are to decide all cases of conscience, and that all goodness is to be measured by the laws of the State.

There is a trace of these errors even in the codes of civil law which enjoy the highest repute. For example, in the code of the Canton Ticino we find: 'Every citizen of the Ticino is born free, and has no bond outside the law' (Art. 17). But the law of the

Canton Ticino cannot dissolve the many ties of conscience binding all human beings equally, and independently of the positive laws of this State.

Even the Austrian code, formed under the influence of great wisdom, seems to have allowed some ambiguity to creep into its definition of civil right. It states: '§1. The complex of laws determining the rights and private obligations of the inhabitants of the State amongst themselves constitutes civil right.' It is certain that 'the private obligations of the inhabitants of the State amongst themselves' are not comprised solely within civil right. There are many obligations which are not, and cannot be, contained in this right.

I realise that some will take this comment as mere pedantry. They will say that the Ticino code clearly speaks of a legal bond, and that the obligations mentioned in the Austrian code are also legal obligations. This is true, but this claim to clarity is not clear to everyone. A proof of this is found in the inveterate error confusing *legality* with *morality*. This error was handed down by the ancient Greek philosophers, passed into Roman laws, and has come down to us. And it is an extremely harmful error (cf. what I have written about it in the *Storia de' sistemi morali*, c. 6).

My own opinion is that here we cannot apply the rule, 'It is useless to speak about things which are present tacitly.' Nor do I think that the words with which such important things as laws are expressed (which often form the sources of ways of thought in a nation) should be inexact or defective. My hope is that the understanding of the reader will render them exact and precise. Finally it needs to be noted carefully that progress in wisdom must consist (and is reduced almost solely to this) in expressing distinctly that which in other ages was not expressed, but understood implicitly both in the decrees of authority and in treatises of philosophy.

The article quoted from the Ticino code has been the subject of some fine comments by the lawyer, G. B. Monti, in his *Secondo saggio di osservazioni sopra alcuni articoli del progetto del Codice Civile*. Mendrisio, 1836.

Index of Biblical References

Numbers in roman indicate paragraphs; numbers in italic indicate footnotes. Bible references are from RSV (Common Bible) unless marked †. In these cases, where the author's use of Scripture is dependent solely upon the Vulgate, the Douai version is used.

Index of Persons

Numbers in roman indicate paragraphs or, where stated, the appendix (app.); numbers in italic indicate footnotes.

General Index

Numbers in roman indicate paragraphs or, where stated, the appendix (app.); numbers in italic indicate footnotes